Principle and Practice:
The Orphan Family

Harriet Martineau

Alpha Editions

This edition published in 2024

ISBN 9789362514981

Design and Setting By
Alpha Editions
www.alphaedis.com
Email - info@alphaedis.com

As per information held with us this book is in Public Domain.
This book is a reproduction of an important historical work.
Alpha Editions uses the best technology to reproduce historical work
in the same manner it was first published to preserve its original nature.
Any marks or number seen are left intentionally to preserve.

Contents

Chapter One.	- 1 -
Chapter Two.	- 14 -
Chapter Three.	- 31 -
Chapter Four.	- 77 -
Chapter Five.	- 85 -

Chapter One.

Let none sit down to read this little tale, whose interest can only be excited by the relation of uncommon circumstances, of romantic adventures, of poetical perplexities, or of picturesque difficulties. No beauties of this kind will be here found. I propose to give a plain, unaffected narrative of the exertions made by a family of young persons, to render themselves and each other happy and useful in the world. The circumstances in which they are placed are so common, that we see persons similarly situated every day: they meet with no adventures, and their difficulties, and the remedies they procure for them, are of so homely a description, as to exclude every exertion of poetical talent in their illustration, and to promise to excite interest in those readers only, who can sympathise with the earnest desires of well-disposed and industrious young persons striving after usefulness, honourable independence, and individual and mutual improvement, amidst real, and not imaginary, discouragements, and substantial, not sentimental, difficulties. I proceed at once to my narrative.

Mr Forsyth was a merchant, who lived in the city of Exeter. He had been a widower for a few years, and had endeavoured to discharge faithfully a parent's duty to five young children, when he too was taken away from those who depended upon him, and whose very existence seemed bound up in his. He was taken from them, and no one knew what would become of these young helpless creatures, who, it was thought, would inherit from their father nothing but his good name, and who possessed nothing but the good principles and industrious habits which his care and affection had imparted to them. They had no near relations, and the friends whom their parents' respectability had gained for them, had families of their own to support, and could offer little but advice and friendly offices: large pecuniary assistance they had it not in their power to impart. One of these friends, who was also Mr Forsyth's executor, took the children into his house till the funeral should be over, and some plans arranged for the future disposal of each of them.

The eldest girl, Jane, was of an age to understand and feel the difficulties which surrounded them. She was sixteen, and from having been her father's *friend* as well as housekeeper, she had a remarkably matured judgment; she was of a thoughtful, perhaps an anxious, disposition, and the loss of her father, together with the anxiety she felt as being now the head of his helpless family, were almost too much for her. Though she was supported by her religious principles, it was with difficulty that she could rouse her mind from dwelling on her perplexities, to form plans, and looking round to see what could be done, and in what way she was to exert her powers for the benefit of her brothers and sisters. She was sometimes oppressed by the thought that the only prospect before her, was a melancholy one of long years of struggles against poverty, and all the grievous evils of dependence. Her brother Charles, who was a year younger than herself, tried with some success to cheer her; he was of an active, enterprising disposition, full of hope and cheerfulness. This disposition subjected him to frequent disappointments, but his father had wisely guarded against their bad effects by forming in him strong habits of perseverance. Charles had been intended by his father for the same business as himself, and he had therefore never been removed from under his parent's eye. It was well now for the whole family that Charles had been so carefully trained. His natural disposition, his acquired habits, and his sense of responsibility, joined to his strong affection for his sisters, made him the object on which Jane fixed her best hopes for the future prosperity of the family. Charles encouraged her hopes, and expressed confidence in his ability to maintain himself at present, and to assist the younger ones when a few years should have matured his powers of usefulness. Jane and Charles anxiously desired some conversation with Mr Barker, the kind friend who had taken them into his house; and were very glad when he invited them, the day after the funeral, to a consultation on the state of their affairs. He told them that it was his intention always to treat them with perfect openness, as it had been their father's custom to do. He was the more inclined to do so, from the knowledge that they were worthy of his confidence, that they possessed prudence beyond their years, and that whatever exertions they might make, would be more efficient if they knew perfectly what they had to do, what objects were to be accomplished, and on what sources they were to depend.

Mr Barker told them that when the affairs were all settled, their income, he feared, would not exceed eighty or ninety pounds a year. That he thought the first object ought to be to give the younger children such an education as would fit them for supporting themselves when they were old enough: that for this purpose the assistance of friends would be required for a few years, and that he knew of some who were willing to assist, believing, from the good principles of the children, that their assistance would be well bestowed, and that their endeavours would be in time rewarded by the usefulness and happiness of those who now required their care.

Jane acquiesced in Mr Barker's proposal, but expressed her hope that they might not be separated. The one thing that she desired more than any other, was, to remain with, and watch over the little ones, and be as far as possible a mother to them. If they were separated, the children would forget her, she said, and that she was sure she could not bear. She did not mind any labour, any privation, any anxieties, if they could but keep together.

"I knew you would think so, my dear," said Mr Barker. "You are perfectly right. You must not be separated, if it can possibly be avoided. I have been consulting with my wife about it, and we have devised a plan for you: but it is yet only a scheme; it is very doubtful whether we can carry it through. I am afraid, however, that Charles must leave you."

"I have been telling Jane, Sir," said Charles, "that I should most likely have to go to some situation where I may maintain myself. I hope, Sir, that that is what you mean."

"And do you think, Charles, that at your age you can work for your own support?"

"Yes, Sir, I do, because others have done it before me. My father taught me enough of business to qualify me for a situation in a merchant's warehouse. At least, he said, only a few weeks ago, that if I was but industrious, I need never be dependent, and that therefore he was easy about me. I hope you think so too, Sir."

"I do, my boy," replied Mr Barker: "as far as skill and industry go, you are to be trusted. But you have not considered, you do not know, the difficulties and dangers which are met with when young men leave their father's house, and go by themselves into the world, especially into the London world, to which you may be destined."

"If you mean temptations to do wrong, Sir," said Charles, "I have been warned by my father about them. But, O, Sir, is it possible, do you think, with all the advantages I have had, with my father's example always before me, with all that is now depending upon me, being, as I am, the brother on whom three sisters rely for support and assistance, is it possible that I should neglect them? that I should disgrace them? that I should forget all my father has done for me? Jane will trust me, I am sure."

He looked towards his sister, and a few proud tears swelled into his eyes.

"No doubt, Charles, your sister feels that she can trust you; and, young as you are, I believe that I can too. But there are many difficulties to be encountered besides direct temptations to crime."

"If I am made fairly to understand, Sir, what is to be required of me, the extent of my trust, I hope I shall meet with no difficulties which honourable principle, industry, and perseverance cannot overcome."

"We will talk more of this, my dear boy, when we have some situation in prospect for you. I hope it may not be difficult to procure one. Your father's name will be a good passport. Then, I hope, I understand that you both approve this first scheme of ours?"

Charles assented at once: Jane, with some exertion to repress her tears.

"And now, my dear Jane, what do you think yourself capable of doing?"

Jane very modestly doubted whether she could do any thing but take care of the children. If they were to live together, she could keep house, she thought, carefully and economically, so as to spend no more than could not possibly be avoided. She thought she could also teach her sisters a little more than she had yet imparted to them: but she hoped, from what Mr Barker had said, that they were to have better teaching than she could give them.

"We have certainly been planning, my dear," said he, "to send Isabella to school, as she is now too old to learn of you only. She is twelve years old, I think?"

"Yes," said Jane; "and Harriet is nine."

"Very well. If Isabella goes to school, Harriet may as well do so too, as the additional expense will not be very great, and may be met by your exertions, if you think as I do about the matter. Your sisters have given you experience in teaching young children, suppose you try your skill again as a daily governess."

Jane was quite willing, if she did but think herself capable of it. Mr Barker thought she had already proved her capability, and advised her, at least, to try the plan.

He told her that a very small house in the outskirts of the town was her father's property. A very little expense would make it habitable for them: furniture was ready, and he could see no objection to their all living in it together. Jane was certainly rather young to become a housekeeper, but the nursemaid, who had lived in the family for some years, was much attached to the children, and had declared her wish to "stay by them," if possible; and Mr Barker had little doubt that she would do all the servant's work of the house, and make their friends tolerably easy with respect to their domestic safety and comfort.

Jane was pleased with the plan, and accordingly it was put in execution with as little delay as possible. In two months' time the house was ready for them. The little furniture and house-linen which was required was put into it, and all the family, except Charles, removed to their new abode. Jane was awfully impressed with the sense of responsibility, when she took her place as mistress of the house, and when she looked upon the three children who depended on her for their domestic comfort, and for much more than this; for guidance in the formation of their habits and characters. But she also felt the great relief of being alone with her brother and sisters, and of having once more a home. The house was tolerably comfortable, though very small. The parlour and kitchen were on the ground floor; over them were two bed-rooms, one of which was occupied by Jane, the other by Isabella and Harriet. Over these were two attics, occupied by little Alfred and the servant. The furniture was scanty, but good of its kind, and likely to last for some years. The only luxurious article in the whole house was a small set of book-shelves, filled with books, which Mr Barker would not allow to be sold off with the other effects. They were not many, but well chosen, and therefore valuable to Jane at present, and likely to be so to her sisters when they should be old enough to make use of them.

Mrs Barker wished that Jane should set out on her new plan of life, as little oppressed by domestic cares as possible, and had therefore assisted her before the removal, in overlooking her own and the children's wardrobe. They were all comfortably supplied with every thing necessary. Their mourning of course was new: perfectly plain, but substantially good, it was intended to last a long time, and that for many months their clothing should be very little expense to them. Jane was an excellent workwoman, and her sister Isabella had been in the habit of assisting her, by keeping her own clothes in very good order. With respect to the little cares of housekeeping, Jane was easy: she had been so well taught, and so long experienced, that she felt herself quite capable of discharging this part of her duty. It was the responsibility of her new office of daily governess which made her most anxious. A situation had been obtained for her, which answered in all respects to Mr Barker's wishes. Jane was to devote six hours a day to the care of her young pupils, who were children of Mr Everett, a surgeon. Mrs Everett was so occupied with the cares of a large family, that she needed assistance, and Jane was to have under her charge four children from the ages of three to twelve: she was to teach them, to superintend in their play hours, and to walk with them. She was to attend from nine till three, and her salary was to be twenty-five pounds a year at first, and afterwards more, if her services were found satisfactory. She stipulated for a fortnight's holiday at Christmas, and also at Midsummer: not for the sake of her own pleasure, but from the fear that her home business would accumulate faster than she could discharge it, so as to render it necessary to devote a short time occasionally to clear it away, and set things straight again. Before she entered on her new engagement, she laid down a plan for the employment of her days, to which she determined to adhere as strictly as possible. It was as follows: for the summer season, which was now approaching, she rose before six o'clock, and set apart two hours for study. Study was absolutely necessary, if she was to keep up, or improve, her ability to teach; and she found that the hours before breakfast were the most quiet and undisturbed that she could devote to this purpose. At eight o'clock the little family assembled in the parlour, to join in prayer, and in reading a short portion of Scripture; after which, they breakfasted. Jane then saw her sisters and little brother off to school, and went into her kitchen to give her household directions before she went out. It was some inconvenience that she could not dine at the same time with the rest of the family; but it could not be helped. The children were obliged to be back at school by two o'clock, and she did not leave Mrs Everett's till three. After dinner, she sat down to her work, of which it may be supposed there was always plenty to be done. The children learned their lessons before tea-time, and after tea they went out to walk all together, whenever the weather would allow of it. They generally returned in time to read a little before nine o'clock, when the younger ones went to bed. The duty of evening, as well as morning prayer was never omitted. Jane sat down to her work again till ten, when she put every thing away, locked up her closets, and went round the house with the servant, to see that all was safe, and as it should be, and then retired to her own room, to enjoy the rest which was fairly earned by the previous hours of activity and usefulness. She was very careful to adhere as closely as possible to the whole of this plan, especially to the hours of walking and going to bed. She was sometimes tempted to think that the children could walk as well without her, and that she was too busy to accompany them: but she never would give way to her inclination to stay at home; for her reason told her that it would be injurious both to herself and her sisters, to give up her accustomed walk. She could not expect to keep up her vigour of mind and body without exercise and relaxation, and it would be wrong to deprive the children of her society in their rambles. A greater temptation still was to sit up late: the quiet hour at night was precious to her; it was the only time she could give to the formation of her plans, and to reflection on her present circumstances and anticipation of the future. The previous exercise of prayer, left her mind in a soothed and tranquil state; and however oppressed, at other times, with fears and cares, this was to her an hour of hope and cheerfulness. She rejoiced that it came at the close of the day, as it enabled her to lay her head on her pillow in that frame of mind which is the best preparation for peaceful sleep and for a cheerful waking. Often was she tempted to prolong this happy hour, but she never did. She was aware of the duty of early rising, and also of taking sufficient rest, and that in order to do both she must keep to the right time of retiring to rest; and accordingly, the moment the clock struck ten, the work was put away, and the train of thought, whatever it might be, was broken off.

The school at which Isabella and Harriet were placed, was one of the best of its kind, and it was not long before a rapid improvement was observed in them both. Isabella's talents were remarkable, but neither herself nor her family were sufficiently aware of this while they received only an irregular and imperfect cultivation. She was remarkably modest, and inclined to be indolent when she had no particular object in view; but set one before her, and her perseverance was unconquerable. She had always been a great reader, and had therefore an excellent stock of general information; but till she went to school, she never could give her attention to any of the drudgery of learning. She wished to learn French and Italian as she had learned her mother-tongue, by *picking up*, instead of beginning at the beginning, and learning grammar. She did *pick up* wonderfully well, to be sure, but she found that would not answer at school. When once convinced of this, she set to work at the grammar with all diligence, and conquered difficulties every day, till she was surprised at her own progress. Her great ambition now was, to make herself a companion for Charles and Jane; not merely to be their friend, but to help them in earning money and obtaining independence, instead of being, as she now was, the most expensive of the family. Jane urged her to be patient, and to think at present of her own improvement only: but she could not help forming many plans for future doings, some reasonable, some much too grand. She had no taste for music, and, by her own desire, therefore, the great expense of musical teaching was not incurred: but drawing was her delight, and she soon made such progress in the art, that Jane was really inspired with her sister's hope that this talent might be turned to good account.

Isabella's very judicious instructress exercised her pupils in composition, and also in translation, much more than is the custom in most schools. To Isabella this was particularly useful; first, in shewing the necessity of accurate knowledge, and her own deficiency in it, and afterwards in serving as a test of her improvement, and, consequently, as an encouragement. She liked this employment much, and soon excelled in it. Her general knowledge was brought into play; and her compositions were, at sixteen, what many at six-and-twenty need not be ashamed of. Her translations were also remarkably spirited and elegant; and a hint from Jane, that this talent might prove useful in the same way as her drawing, was quite sufficient to insure Isabella's particular exertions in its improvement.

Mr and Mrs Barker called frequently to see their young friends, and they never quitted the door without leaving happy and grateful hearts behind them. They rewarded Jane's exertions with something better than praise—with their friendship and confidence. Mr Barker talked to her about her affairs without any reserve, and the gratitude this excited in her was great. Her kind friend told her, one day, that Mr Rathbone, an old friend of her father's, who lived in London, had been enquiring about the family of Mr Forsyth, and, on hearing of their circumstances; had expressed his desire of being useful to them. "I told him, my dear," said Mr Barker, "that his kind offices would be more acceptable by and by than at present. We now see our way clear for two years, I hope; and it is well to keep a stock of kindness in reserve, to be drawn upon in case of need."

Jane expressed her gratitude for the kindness which had assisted them thus far, and said she feared she must make up her mind to be a burden to her friends for some time to come; but she could answer for her brothers and sisters, as well as herself, that no exertion on their part should be wanting.

"So we see already, my dear," said Mr Barker. "Mr Rathbone made enquiry about each of you; and I sent him, in return, a full description of you all. I think it most likely that he will keep his eye upon Alfred, and that whatever he may do hereafter will be for him."

"I am sure," said Jane, "Mr Rathbone's kindness is most unlooked for; for it must be many years since he has known our family. I have heard my father speak of him, but I do not remember ever to have seen him."

"It is only two years," replied Mr Barker, "since he returned from India, where he passed twenty years, losing his health, and growing immensely rich. He tells me that he was under considerable obligations to your good father for some exertions on his behalf during his absence; but of what nature these exertions were he does not say. Well, my dear, I must be going. Have you any thing more to say to me? Is all comfortable here, and as you like it?"

"Quite, Sir, thank you: we are only too comfortable for our circumstances, I am afraid."

"No, no, my dear; I hope Hannah and you go on comfortably together. Your house looks very neat and orderly," said he, looking round him. "Is that her doing or yours?"

"All Hannah's doing. We could not be better or more respectfully served, if we were as rich as Mr Rathbone. But I grieve to think that such a servant should make such sacrifices for us; she would be prized in any house."

"Depend upon it, Jane, she will find her reward in time. I am much mistaken if she does not find it now, day by day. You will be prosperous one day, and then she will share your prosperity, you know."

"We will hope so," said Jane. "Will you thank Mr Rathbone, Sir, for us, or shall I write myself?"

"No occasion at all, my dear, I am obliged to write to him to-morrow on business. Good-bye to you."

About a week after this, as the young people were busily employed, as usual, before tea, Jane mending stockings, Isabella translating French, Harriet learning geography, and Alfred frowning over his Latin grammar, Hannah brought in a large box, which had just arrived from London by the carrier, carriage paid. It must be a mistake, Jane thought; but no, it was not a mistake, the direction was plain and full: "Miss Forsyth, Number 21, South Bridge Street, Exeter." The stockings and books were thrown aside, and the whole family adjourned to the kitchen, to open the wonderful box. After the removal of several sheets of paper, a letter appeared at the top, addressed to Jane. She hastily opened it, and read as follows:

> "My dear young Friend,—
>
> "You must allow me thus to address you, though you have never seen me, and probably have never heard of me. My husband's old friendship with your father

is, however, a sufficient ground for the establishment of an intercourse between us, which may be advantageous to you, and I am sure will be very pleasant to us. We owe too much to your excellent father, not to desire to be of use, if possible, to his children. I cannot tell you now, but if we ever meet, you shall know how deep is the debt of gratitude due to the friend who incurred difficulty and hazard for the sake of our interests, and who, for many weeks and months, was subjected to anxiety and fatigue on our account, when we were in India, not aware of our obligations to him, and therefore unable to express or to testify our gratitude. That friend was your father. You must accept our good offices, my dear young friend, and tell us how we can be useful to you. Mr Barker tells us that our assistance will be more acceptable hereafter than at present. Remember, then, if you please, that we expect to be applied to whenever you can give us the pleasure of serving you, or any of your family. In the mean time, we hope that the contents of this box will be useful to you, and that its arrival will afford as much pleasure to your young brother and sisters, as I remember experiencing in my childhood from similar accidents.

"I am not one, Miss Forsyth, who can reconcile it to myself to gain the affections of young people by flattery; but I cannot withhold the encouragement of an expression of approbation, when I really feel it to be deserved by the exercise of self-denial and honourable industry. I am told that you are now earning such approbation from all who feel an interest in you. Believe, therefore, that it is with as much sincerity as good-will, that Mr Rathbone and myself add the word *respect* to the affection with which we subscribe ourselves,—

"Your friends,—

"F. and S. Rathbone."

Jane had escaped to the parlour almost as soon as she began this letter, and her eyes were so dimmed by tears that she could scarcely proceed. Isabella, who was far more anxious about Jane and the letter, than about the box, immediately followed her, and they finished it together. Isabella was almost as much pleased, quite as much touched, with the part which concerned Jane, as with that which respected her father. She kissed her affectionately, and rejoiced that others were aware of her merit; others who could encourage it as it deserved, and reward it better than those in whose behalf her self-denial and industry were exerted.

In the mean time Alfred and Harriet were extremely impatient to proceed with the examination of the box, but Hannah would not allow it till Jane and Isabella were present. They soon returned to the kitchen, and it would be difficult to say whose countenance exhibited the most astonishment as the various presents were brought forth to view. A little card-paper box, well stuffed with cotton-wool, contained a handsome plain gold watch, which, with its seal and key, were intended for Jane. A drawing-box, well fitted up with colours and pencils of all kinds, and accompanied with a large quantity of drawing-papers, and two sketch-books, was directed to Isabella. A pretty writing-desk, filled with all the comforts and luxuries which can appertain to that pretty article of furniture, bore Harriet's name; as did also a large quantity of music, which astonished her not a little, as, though she much wished it, she had not yet begun to learn, and had no prospect of such an indulgence for a long time to come. Her sisters thought it a very likely mistake for Mrs Rathbone to make: as one sister drew, she might easily imagine that another played. But Harriet could not help hoping that, *some how or other*, it was to come to pass, that she should learn music directly. And she was right, as we shall see. Imagination came nearer the truth than reason, for once.

By this time Alfred began to be dismayed lest there should be no present for him; but Hannah had not yet got to the bottom of the box. When she had, she took out several packages of books, two of them directed to Alfred, and the others to the Miss Forsyths. Alfred's present consisted of some beautiful editions of the classics, so valuable that the owner of them was likely to be long before he understood how rich he was in their possession. There was also a large cake directed to him, to which he was disposed to pay a more immediate attention than to his books. The girls found that their library was to be enriched by the best foreign editions of Tasso and Alfieri, and of Racine, and by a beautiful edition of Shakspeare. They were bewildered by the splendour of these presents, so far exceeding in value any thing they had before possessed. Their usual tea hour was long past before they thought of any thing but the wonderful box. At length, however, they determined to finish their meal as quickly as possible, and to go and tell their kind friends, the Barkers, of their good fortune. It was vain to think of putting their riches out of sight, so the watch was hung over the chimney-piece, the desk, drawing-box, and books, stuck up wherever room could be made for them. While they were at tea, however, Mr and Mrs Barker called, probably with some suspicion of what they were to see, for Mr Barker glanced round the room as he entered it. "Why, young ladies," said he, "you are so splendid I dare not come in, I am afraid. My dear, we have nothing like this to shew at home. What good fairy can have done all this?"

"Two good fairies from India have sent us these beautiful things, Sir," said Isabella.

"From India! I did not know you had any such acquaintance in India."

"From India, by way of London, Sir," said Jane, "now you can guess."

"Yes, yes, my dear, I know well enough. I had some idea of finding an exhibition when I came to-night, but not such a one as this, I own. Alfred, my boy, how comes your cake to be on this chair, instead of on the tea-table?"

"We are not going to cut it to-night, Sir."

"I hardly know when we shall," said Jane. "It is too large to eat it all ourselves."

"It does look very good, to be sure," said Mr Barker. "My mouth waters when I look at it."

Isabella ran for a knife to cut it directly, but Mr Barker stopped her. "Not now, my dear; but I hoped you would have asked us to tea, to taste your cake."

"And will you really come, Sir?" asked Jane. "Mrs Barker, will you come to-morrow, and drink tea with us? And the children too. We have no amusement to offer but the cake: but we shall be quite delighted if you will come."

"With all my heart, Jane. We and two of the children will come, and we will take a long walk afterwards if you please. We shall have more time to look at your presents than we have now; we cannot stay longer to-night."

Jane put Mrs Rathbone's letter into Mr Barker's hand, and he went aside to read it. He returned it to her in silence. She obtained Mr Rathbone's address, that she might, this very evening, write her thanks for his munificent kindness.

When their friends were gone, the young people found it was too late to take their usual walk; besides, their lessons were not finished, and they resolutely sat down to their business: Alfred, with the fear of the bottom of the class before his eyes; Harriet, with the mixed motive of this fear, and the wish to do right; Isabella, influenced by the wish alone. Alfred asked Jane to hear him his lesson, and the two words, "quite perfect," at length repaid his labours.

"But, Jane," said Alfred, "you have two watches now; you will not want them both."

"Certainly," said Jane. "Isabella shall have the old one; she will value it as having been my mother's; though it is not a very serviceable one."

"O! thank you, Jane," said Isabella. "I had not thought of such a thing, I am sure. I had no idea of having a watch for many years to come."

"If you will undertake to get Harriet and Alfred off to bed, Isabella, I will. And a watch-pocket for you. Or you can make one in an hour. Sit up with me for this one evening, and we will consult what to do with our books; and I will write my letter before breakfast to-morrow: my head will be clearer then."

No sooner said than done. The girls found room in a closet for their shabbiest books, and in the morning the new ones were installed in their places on the shelves, much to the satisfaction of their owners. Jane's letter was written and dispatched, and she was more comfortable when she had attempted to express her gratitude to her father's faithful friends, though she felt that nothing she could say could do justice to her feelings. When she had put her letter into the post-office, she turned her attention from the subject, that her head might not be running on other things when she ought to be attending to her pupils.

They all got forward with their business this day, that they might be ready with a clear conscience to receive their friends on the first occasion when they had to exercise hospitality. Isabella found her watch a prodigious assistance, she declared.

The Barkers enjoyed the evening as much as their young host and hostesses. The weather was charming, the country looked beautiful, the children were merry, and, "though last, not least," the cake was delicious.

Chapter Two.

"But where is Charles all this time?" my readers will ask. Charles is in London, endeavouring to discharge, to the best of his ability, the duties of a situation which had been procured for him in the warehouse of a general merchant, who had had dealings with Mr Forsyth, had always esteemed him for his integrity, and was, therefore, willing to make trial of the services of the youth who had been brought up under the eye of such a father.

Charles found his situation a laborious one; and his salary was so small that he could only by great frugality subsist upon it himself. He found that he must wait till his character had been tried, and till he grew older, before he could afford any substantial assistance to his family. His state of mind and circumstances will be better understood from his letters to Jane, than from any account we could give. Here, therefore, are some of them, with Jane's answers.

> "My dearest Jane,—
>
> "I am glad that the day appointed for writing has arrived: you cannot conceive the comfort your letters are to me, and the pleasure I have in answering them. I suppose that in time I shall get accustomed to the silence I am now obliged to observe with respect to the subjects I love most to talk upon; but I sigh sometimes for some one to whom I can speak of my father, and of times past; or of you, and time present, and to come. My companions here are good-tempered enough, and we go on smoothly and easily together, and I know that this is a great thing to be able to say; and that many in my situation would be glad to say as much: but yet I cannot help feeling the want of some friend to whom I can speak of what is nearest to my heart, and there is not one person in this wide city who knows you, or who could possibly feel much interest in hearing me talk of you. Consequently I hold my tongue, and your name has never passed my lips since we parted. But, dearest Jane, my thoughts of you are all the more frequent and the more dear, on this account; and on this account, I feel the more deeply, the privilege of

opening my heart to the One friend who loves you better than any mortal can, who cares for your interests, more than any earthly friend can care, and who can provide for them when I can do nothing but love you, and pray for you. I continually determine that I will not be anxious about you; that we will all trust and be cheerful; and I generally keep my resolution. I hope you do the same. Whatever anxious thoughts you may have, must be for yourselves: you may be quite easy about me. I am well, very busy, and of course very cheerful; my comfort is attended to, and I have nothing to complain of in any body near me. I enjoy many privileges, and shall be able to make more for myself, when I become better acquainted with my situation. In short, the present is very tolerably comfortable, I have the prospect of increasing comforts, and may in time do grand things for you, as well as for myself. You shake your head as you read this, I dare say: but I do not see why, by industry, I may not do as grand things as others have done before me; especially as I am blessed with good friends at my setting out, which is an immense advantage to begin with. To shew you that I am not dreaming about any *luck* happening to me, and that I only mean to depend on skill and industry for my prosperity, if I ever am to be prosperous, I will tell you how I spend my three hours in the evening—I am actually hard at work at the French and Spanish grammar. Yes, at grammar! though, I dare say, that is the last thing you would have thought of my applying to. I want to rise, as fast as possible, from trust to trust, in this house, and it can only be done by duly qualifying myself: so I mean to learn first every thing requisite for the proper discharge of the most responsible situation of all; and then, if I have time left, I will learn other things, to which my wishes begin to tend, for the sake of general cultivation and enlargement of mind; which, I am convinced, is as great an advantage to the man of business, as to the professional man, or the private gentleman. I will tell you always how far I am able to carry my plans into execution, and you will give me what encouragement and assistance you can. I wonder whether you like Mrs Everett as well as I like Mr Gardiner. He is a most kind friend to me on the whole: I say 'on the whole,' because there is the drawback of a fault of temper, which will occasionally try my patience; but this is all. I should not have mentioned it, except that I wish you to know every particular of my situation, and that, I am sure, what I say goes no further, at least where *character* is concerned. Mr Gardiner makes a point of speaking to me every day, and seems to like to call me by my surname, doubtless because it was my father's. One day he called me Alfred Forsyth: he begged my pardon, and said he had been used to that name. He has asked me to dine with him next Sunday. This is very kind of him, I am sure.

"Now, Jane, be sure you tell me every thing about yourself, and the other dear girls, and Alfred. Every little trifling particular is pleasant to read about. I am very glad that Isabella's drawing prospers so well: I wish she may be able to send me a drawing soon; it would be quite a treasure to me. May I not see some of her hand-writing in the next letter? There is only one thing more I wish particularly to say. I entreat you, my dearest sister, not to work too hard or too anxiously. Take care of your health and spirits as you value ours. Give my best love to all at home, and my affectionate respects to Mr and Mrs Barker, if they will accept them. I am, dearest Jane,—

"Your most affectionate,—

"Charles Forsyth.

"Remember me kindly to Hannah."

From Jane to Charles.

"Exeter, September 5th.

"Dear Charles,—

"We all thank you for your long letter. It has made us, on the whole, easy and comfortable about you. As long as you are as active and enterprising as you are now, you will be happy, for I believe that the grand secret of happiness consists in having a good pursuit, which can be followed with some success. To ensure this success, the pursuit must be rational; and I assure you, that so far from shaking my head at your hopes of doing 'grand things,' I think your hopes are very rational, provided that by 'grand things,' you and I mean the same. I suppose you mean no more than that, by qualifying yourself for higher situations than the one which you now hold, you hope to rise in rank and riches high enough to assist your family, and to enable them to work in the same manner for their own independence hereafter. This prospect is quite grand enough for us at present. We must never dream of being very rich; I am afraid that we must not even hope to discharge our very heavy obligations to our friends in any other way than by our gratitude, and by making the best use of their kindness. The weight of obligation sits heavy on me: I am afraid I am proud, and therefore it may be well for me that I am obliged to submit to dependence; but I will never rest till I can relieve our friends from a charge which extreme kindness has induced them to take upon themselves, but which must in time become burdensome. How happy should I be to do any kind of service to any of them! Amidst the chances and changes of the world, who knows but we may? But I must not think and write in this way. We must cheerfully and willingly, as well as most gratefully, accept the kindness which they so cheerfully and willingly offer. We go on very comfortably on the whole. We work very hard, but not more so than is good for body and mind, as you would be convinced if you could see how well we look and how happy we are together. The only unpleasant circumstance which has occurred lately, is a misunderstanding between Mrs Everett and myself. I really cannot tell you, for I do not know myself, what it was about; but she was, for two or three days, so dissatisfied with me, that I was afraid of being obliged to give up my charge. I told no one of it, but determined to bear it quietly for a few days, and to do my best for the children, and see whether matters would not come round again. My plan answered: we go on tolerably smoothly again, though not so very comfortably as before. I must recollect, however, that in my inexperience I may commit errors in my management of the children, and that Mrs Everett may justly feel that she has something to bear with in me. I wish, however, that she would tell me the causes of her discontent, and then the evil might be remedied without any ill-will on either side. Before this time, she was as kind as possible, and will be so again, I hope. I cannot help seeing that the children improve, and I have the satisfaction of knowing that Mr Everett thinks so too. He told Mr Barker so, and I think I could have guessed it from his manner towards me.

"Isabella desires her best love to you, and she will send you a drawing by the first opportunity that offers. She has sketched your favourite Bubbling Spring for the purpose, thinking you would like it better than any other subject. I am sure you would think it beautiful, independently of the sweet associations which endear that spot peculiarly to us. I am really astonished at Isabella's progress in drawing: her pencil sketches are beautiful, and she succeeds as well or better in water-colours. She finishes very highly in the latter, and yet she is quick. If she spent as much time as many girls do on her drawing, I should not think it right to let her sacrifice other things to this accomplishment, though it is useful and beautiful, and may, she hopes, be turned to some good account. Harriet and Alfred are as good as children can be. Their affection is delightful to me. It is quite sufficient to repay all my cares for them. They get on very well at school, though at their age their progress cannot be so remarkable as Isabella's.

"Isabella is now come into the room, and she begs to fill the little that remains of this sheet. She has a very fine subject to write about, which I kept to the last, as being the most remarkable event which has happened to us for a very long time. Farewell, my dearest brother, we think of you hourly, and one of our greatest delights is to talk over the probabilities of our meeting. O, when will it be?

"Ever your affectionate,—

"Jane Forsyth."

The subject on which Isabella wrote to her brother, was that of Mr and Mrs Rathbone's noble present. As my readers are already acquainted with the circumstances, there is no occasion to weary them with a repetition. We also omit three or four of Charles's letters, which contain no detail of new events, and proceed to one which he wrote on Christmas-day.

"Dear Jane,—

"I address this letter to you, merely because I can express myself better when writing to one person than to several; but the contents of this are wholly, or in part, as you may see fit, for the public good: by the public, meaning the inhabitants of Number 21, South Bridge Street. In the first place, I offer you all my love, and best wishes for a cheerful Christmas, and much enjoyment of your holidays. I am afraid, dear Jane, that your holidays will be somewhat busy ones; but you have Isabella to help you to make 'a clearance of business,' as you say. I do not know what you will say to me for providing more work for you. I will explain presently what I mean by this. I hope the beautiful bright sun of this happy day brings as much cheerfulness to your hearts as it does to mine. There is no day of the year which so forcibly reminds us of the great number and magnitude of our blessings as this; and consequently there is no day on which we can feel so happy. I am more impressed than ever with this feeling to-day. It is the first Christmas-Day that I have ever passed away from home; but so far from this making me melancholy, I am most happy in the full tide of affection which is flowing towards you all, and not less so, in the overflowing gratitude which I feel toward that Parent who has blessed us in each other, in the love which is our happiness here, and which, we hope, will make our joy hereafter. God bless you all, and make you as happy as I wish you to be; as happy as I am at this moment.

"I can quite imagine how you will spend this day. You will take a long walk, and enjoy a long talk, in which I hope to come in for a share; though, alas!

too far off to have the benefit of what you are saying. You will go to church, and I think I know what your feelings will be there. The rest of the day will be spent at Mr Barker's, I conjecture: but will good Hannah be at home alone? I am going to dine at Mr Rathbone's, but as they dine late, I shall have time for a long walk after church. You cannot imagine, no one who has not lived in London can imagine, the delight of a country walk to me. I rejoice that the day is so fine. Mr Gardiner was so kind as to ask me to dine with him to-day: so you see there was no danger of my being solitary, much less, melancholy.

"But now to my business, for even to-day I have business to write about. You know when I arrived here, at Midsummer, Mr Gardiner paid me my first quarter's salary in advance: he bid me not mention the circumstance, for fear of others expecting the same favour. He said at the same time, that he hoped I would make a friend of him in case of any difficulty which might occur in money matters, as I was, he thought, very young to manage for myself on a small salary. Knowing that I was necessarily at some unusual expense on my first arrival, he has frequently asked whether I wanted any assistance. I have always said, no; for I have been really well off. Mr Barker sent me up with ten pounds in my pocket, after my travelling expenses were paid, and this, with my quarter's salary, has been more than sufficient for me. Besides this I have the ten pound note that Mr Rathbone gave me still unchanged, so that I have every reason to hope that I shall get on till Midsummer, without taking any more money of Mr Gardiner; and from that time, I shall take my salary half-yearly. Now, I think, I have found a very good occasion for changing my note: I hope you and Isabella will approve of my plan; as it is intended for your advantage, I am anxious that it should succeed. I had occasion to go last week, on some business of Mr Gardiner's, to a large toy-shop in Holborn, and while I was waiting to speak to the owner, I saw the shopman unpack a basket, which seemed to have arrived from the country. It contained a great variety of work-bags and boxes, card-racks, and such things, ornamented in various ways; many of them with drawings. When I had finished my business, I enquired whether a ready sale could be found for such articles, and what would be the probable success, if some friends of mine, who could draw very well, were to send up some specimens of their talents, like those on the counter. The owner of the shop, Mr Blyth, said, that he found it easy to obtain a supply of such articles, but that the best and prettiest would always command the best sale. He told me I might, if I chose, shew him what my friends could do, and that if their work was approved he might employ them occasionally; but of course could promise nothing at present. Now, my dear girls, I think you might make a little money these holidays by trying your hand on these things: you, Isabella, can draw all kinds of pretty things; and you, Jane, can make up the bags, etcetera, very neatly. Let me know, by the next post, whether you are inclined to try, and I will send you a few patterns and materials. I have the opportunity of getting remnants of coloured silk and ribbon cheap; so cheap that you need not grudge the carriage of them. Suppose you make at first, with all your skill and care, about a dozen bags, and netting-cases, and card-racks; and pray, Isabella, let one of your card-racks have a sketch of the Bubbling Spring on it, and another the cottage at the foot of Elston Hill. Do not scruple, my dear girls, on account of the risk, the very little risk to be incurred. If our scheme answers, I promise you that you shall repay me; if not, I can spare the small sum needed. Let me know exactly how your accounts stand this Christmas, and be easy and hopeful, whatever may happen. I wanted to say a great deal about Mr and Mrs Rathbone, but it is just time for church, and I must close my letter. I can write again by the parcel, if you authorise me to send it.—Farewell, my very dear sisters and brother.

"I am your most affectionate,—

"Charles Forsyth."

"What a comfortable letter!" exclaimed Jane, as she finished it. "Dear Charles is as happy as we are!"

"And just as kind as ever," said Isabella: "he will never be spoiled by living in London. He will never forget, or be ashamed of us. How ready he is to set his head and hands to work in our service! But we are to write by this day's post our answer to this proposal: what shall we do, Jane?"

"Try, by all means, I think," said Jane. "What do you say, Isabella?"

"Try, by all means, I say too, and I have very little doubt of success. The sooner we begin the better, so we will write immediately. I think Mr Barker will not disapprove of it."

"Certainly not," said Jane. "But, if you please, we will tell no one about it till we see whether the plan answers or not. I am not fond of a hasty communication of plans; and besides, I wish that our friends, instead of considering us as schemers, should see, that, while we form plans, we have patience and industry to carry them through, or that they should know nothing of the matter. When we can go with earned money in our hands to Mr Barker, we will tell him how we got it: in the mean while, we will not trouble him, or run the risk of interruption ourselves."

"Very right," said Isabella. "What shall we do about Harriet and Alfred? May we tell them?"

"I think they must know," replied Jane. "You must make use of the day-light for your drawing, and they must see what you are doing. We must trust them. It will be a good lesson in keeping a secret."

The whole plan was soon settled. The letter was dispatched to Charles, and, by the earliest possible hour, the parcel with its pretty contents arrived. Charles had most completely supplied all the necessary materials, so that there were no purchases to be made, and nothing hindered their setting immediately to work. During the first evening Jane and Isabella very carefully cut paper patterns from the articles which were sent as patterns, and marked them very exactly on the pasteboard before they cut it. When the different sides of the bags, etcetera, were cut out they were found to fit exactly; so that so far all was right. This was all that they could do by candle-light, and Isabella longed for the morning that she might begin her drawing. She was pleased to see that the drawings on the pattern bags did not nearly equal what she was capable of doing, though Charles had said that he purposely picked out those which appeared to him the best done.

The next morning breakfast was soon over, and the table placed in the best light by the window. Isabella was seated at her drawing, Jane at work beside her, and the children at their amusements, very carefully avoiding the table, lest they should shake it and spoil Isabella's drawing. They were proud of their secret, and it was to be part of their business to watch and give notice of the approach of any uninitiated person, from whose sight all tale-telling materials were to be quickly swept away.

By two hours before dinner one beautiful little drawing was finished. It was duly admired, and Jane congratulated her sister on the success of her first day's exertion; but she was surprised to see Isabella sitting down to begin another. "My dear Isabella, you have done for to-day, surely?"

"No, Jane; I must outline another. I can finish the outline and the first shades before dinner."

"But when do you mean to walk? You do not, surely, mean to stay at home this beautiful day?"

"Only this one day: you can do without me this one day. I cannot leave off now, indeed."

"O, Isabella, how often have I gone with you when I had much more necessary things than these trifles to do at home! Depend upon it, you will not do the second so well as the first, if you sit so long at it; you will bring on a headache, too, and make me sorry that Charles ever devised this plan for us."

"Do put it by, Isabella," said Harriet, "and go with us."

"I will, directly," said Isabella. "I beg your pardon, Jane; I was selfish, and you never are. There, they are locked up till to-morrow, and now let us make haste, and go for our walk."

When Isabella had done a few drawings, and became more accustomed to the employment, she found that she need not be so absorbed in it, as to be unable to attend to her sisters while they read aloud. This added great pleasantness to their morning employment, and both Jane's work, and Isabella's drawing, got on fast while they listened to Harriet and Alfred, who took it in turn to read. But when the pasting together of their work began, there was an end of reading. It was too anxious a business to admit of any division of attention. The gilt edges must be exactly even, the sides must go exactly together, the bottoms must be exactly flat; or they would be deformed and unsteady. Jane was the only one careful enough to undertake this most difficult part of the business, and she bestowed great pains upon it. In general, she completely succeeded; but it was a work of time, and the fortnight of her holidays was over before their task was more than two-thirds done. Eight articles out of the dozen were finished, and she longed to see them completed. It was with a sigh that she left the busy and happy party at home, on the morning when she resumed her charge at Mrs Everett's, and she could not help fancying that Mrs Everett was less kind than usual, that the children were far from improved by their release from her authority, that they had never been so troublesome, and her task never so irksome. This was in part true; the children were nearly as unwilling to be managed, as Jane was to manage them, and they were fully as sorry as she, that the days of lessons and work, of authority and obedience, were come again, after the romping hours of their Christmas revellings.

A strong effort at patience on Jane's part, and something like an endeavour to be good on the children's, soon restored things to their usual state, and teacher and learners were on their old terms again. When Jane returned home, she found that Isabella had put away her drawing in time to take Harriet and Alfred a walk before dinner. The evening was passed busily and happily, and the finishing stroke was put to two more of the bags and baskets. In a week more all were completed. Jane was glad of it. The last two or three drawings had not been quite so well done, and it was easy to see that Isabella began to be tired. She owned that she was a little, a very little; but said, that, after a week's rest, she should be able to begin again with as much relish as ever. Jane was sorry that she had worked so hard, and recommended her to think no more of drawing for the rest of the holidays. Ten days only now remained before school should begin again; and Isabella passed the time very happily between books, walking, and work. We must not forget, also, a long letter which she wrote to Charles, by the box which carried their work. It will be in vain to guess at the hopes and fears, the alternate confidence and anxiety which these industrious girls felt about the probable reward of their labours. They calculated the number of days which must pass before a letter from Charles could arrive, to bid them rejoice or be patient yet longer. They told each other continually that they were looking for a letter too soon; that it was not likely they should have an answer till the things were sold. Their kind brother could imagine their anxiety, and the very first moment that he could send them intelligence of their success he did so, in the following letter.

"My dear Girls,—

"I hope I have not disappointed you by delaying my letter for a few days, but I thought it would be quite a pity to write till I could give you Mr Blyth's opinion, and that of the public, about your works. I have just been to the shop, and though it is late at night, I cannot go to bed till I have offered you my congratulations. I have in my pocket three guineas, which Mr Blyth thinks a fair price for your work. I hope you will think so too, and be as well satisfied with your gains as I am. Mr Blyth gave me an order for as many more as you like to send up, for he has eyes to see that your things are prettier, and better made, than any articles of the kind in his shop. I hope you will be encouraged by your deserved success, and that the next parcel you send will keep up your credit. I know you cannot get on so fast when the holidays are over. Indeed I scarcely know how you will find time at all; but as you desire me to send you more work, I conclude you will make time for it some how or other. Your leisure hours can hardly be better spent, I think; and I have no fear but that you should overwork yourselves. That you will neglect your duties of teaching and learning, I never, for a moment, supposed; so your assurances on that head, my dear girls, are quite unnecessary. Now, pray take care of your health and spirits: take exercise and amusement, and remember that there is not the least hurry in the world for these things. If they are not finished till Midsummer, it will be of much less consequence than your over-working yourselves. I do not send you the money. I can get your materials so very cheap that the carriage of them will answer again. I have, according to your desire, paid myself: so now you stand on your own ground, and are, in this matter, under no obligations to any body, not even to your own brother; so I hope my proud sisters will be satisfied. I laid out only eighteen shillings. I have taken that sum from your three guineas, and will lay out the remainder in silk, ribbon, paper, etcetera. It is pleasanter, I know, to see money at once, than materials for further work; but I think your present success, and especially your darling independence, will afford you pleasure enough for this time, and that you will be willing to wait awhile for more substantial gains. You deserve all you can get, my dear girls, and I am sure you cannot desire success so earnestly, or rejoice in it so heartily, as I do for you. My concerns prosper: that is, I am busy, well, and cheerful, and independent. Some little rubs I meet with, like any body else; but I wonder sometimes to think how happy I am. Anxious thoughts for you sadden me now and then; but I try to remember, that the same kind Parent who has hitherto protected us, is still about our path, and that we have nothing to do but to labour and trust. We are doing now what we can, and therefore we ought to be satisfied with the present and hopeful for the future, and grateful, day by day, hour by hour.

"Your last letter was written in such a spirit of cheerfulness, that if I had been miserable, I could not have shut my heart against its influence: but I was not miserable. I was sitting alone, my thoughts far from myself, from you, from every body; for I was absorbed in a Spanish book which I was translating. You may imagine how readily it was thrown aside when the postman knocked at the door, and how joyously the full tide of my thoughts turned towards home, and how my affection rested on each of you in turn, and blessed each of your names as it rose, accompanied with a thousand sweet recollections, to my remembrance. I hope you will give me the pleasure of such another evening soon. I met Mr Rathbone in the street the other day. He enquired how you all were, and said I must go and dine with him soon, as he has something to say to me. He says that he has requested Mr Barker to allow Harriet to learn music, as he hears she has a taste for it. He hopes that dear Harriet will come to London some time or other and play to him, as music is his passion. I cannot describe to you how kind his manner is, nor how dearly I love the very sight of this good man. And yet even he does not escape slander. I have heard it said, often and often, that he is a perfect tyrant to his inferiors, that as long as he is treated with deference, he is unwearied in kindness, but that the least opposition enrages him, and that once displeased he is an irreconcilable enemy. Of course I believe nothing of all this, and have shewn no little indignation when I have heard such things said.

What a world it must be, when such a man as Mr Rathbone is slandered! I do not intend to be curious about what he has to say to me till the time comes. Perhaps he will tell me what was the nature of the service which my dear father rendered him. But I will not think more of the matter: it may be only a trifle after all.

"I am very sorry to conclude, but I must be off to bed; it is very late, and I must be at the warehouse two hours sooner than usual to-morrow. I hope you will be satisfied with what I send you, and that Harriet will be pleased at her musical prospects. Farewell, all of you; let me hear soon, and believe me,—

"Your very affectionate brother,—

"Charles Forsyth.

"P.S. I have now received a note from Mr Rathbone, in which he says that he and Mrs R. are obliged to leave town for some weeks: and that therefore they must defer seeing me at present. He asks whether Alfred has ever shewn any taste for mathematics, and expresses his hope that his attention will be directed that way without delay. What can this mean? You had better ask Mr Barker."

Mr Barker was no better able to guess Mr Rathbone's designs than Charles himself; so they were all obliged to wait in patience till their kind friend should return to town, which did not take place till the following autumn. In the mean time, however, his directions were observed, and Alfred began to learn mathematics.

Jane and Isabella had so little time now for the employment which their brother had provided for them, that March was past before another box was prepared for Mr Blyth. Their brother had the pleasure of transmitting five guineas to them, as the reward of their industry; and we may imagine the complacency and satisfaction with which they revealed the history of their labours and earnings to their friend Mr Barker. He was as much pleased as they expected, and even more surprised. He asked them how they intended to apply the money. They replied without hesitation, to the children's school expenses; for their only object was to make themselves less burdensome to their friends. Mr Barker would not allow of this. He recommended them to lay by their earnings as a separate fund, to be applied when any extraordinary occasion should arise. He kindly added, that money so earned should bring some pleasure in its expenditure to those who had obtained it by industry, and that he did not see why their parlour should not in time be graced by a pair of globes, or even a piano, honourably obtained by their own exertions. This was a splendid prospect, and an animating one for these good girls, and they determined to set to work again, as soon as the holidays should afford them leisure. It was now necessary, however, to try their hands at something else, as Mr Blyth had given notice that it would be some months before he should want a further supply of the articles on which they had hitherto so profitably employed their ingenuity.

What should they next attempt? This was a difficult question to answer, and the girls determined to look about them, and observe, and wait for the present, and not expect to earn more money before the holidays. So they spent their leisure time through April and May in reading and drawing for improvement, and in work, of which their hands were always full.

When Midsummer came, and Jane made up her accounts at the close of her first year of housekeeping, she thought she had every reason to be satisfied and grateful. She had the encouragement also of Mr Barker's warm approbation of her self-denying industry, and of her excellent management. He gave her encouragement of another kind also. He told her that Mr Everett had expressed his entire satisfaction in her conduct to the children under her care, and his intention of either raising her salary, or doing something equivalent to this, at the end of the next year. The lady whose school Isabella and Harriet attended, also spoke in praise of the girls to Mr Barker, and told him that their good principles, their influential sense of religion, which was evinced by their uniform good conduct, afforded a certain proof of excellent management at home. She made many enquiries concerning Jane, and determined to keep her eye on her, and to find some opportunity of doing service to one who so well merited kindness and assistance. Mr Barker did not tell Jane all this; but he told her enough to cause tears of pleasure to swell into her eyes, and emotions of unspeakable gratitude to arise in her heart. She reserved the expression of this gratitude till, alone in her chamber, she could pour out her whole soul before Him who had directed and upheld her steps on the narrow path of duty, and who was now showering rich blessings upon her, and filling her heart with peace and hope. She thanked him that he had preserved them to each other, and yet more, that their family peace was unbroken: that they were closely united in the love of Him and of each other. She felt that as long as this love subsisted she could bear any trials that came from without; and though she looked forward to probable anxieties and difficulties, the prospect did not dismay her, so strong did she now feel in an Almighty support, and in perfect reliance on the goodness and mercy which was now about her, and which, she trusted, would follow her all the days of her life. It was not indeed to be expected that every year should pass away so smoothly. They had all enjoyed health and comfort at home, improvement and pleasure abroad. They had gained new friends, and so far from suffering want, their affairs bore a more cheering aspect than they could have hoped. Their income amounted, as I have said, to eighty pounds a year, and they had besides a house of their own. They had been at scarcely any expense for clothes, and their good servant Hannah had very low wages. Their expenditure this year, under Jane's excellent management, was only fifty-six pounds: the rest of their income, with Jane's salary of twenty-five pounds, went therefore towards the fund which their friends had raised for the education of the three younger ones. Charles managed to be independent, as we know, and Isabella hoped that in four or five years she might be so too. Jane never expected to spend so little again. She could not hope that their house would be always so free from sickness, or that their wants would always be so few.

Mr Barker, after examining her accounts, and praising the accuracy with which they were kept, congratulated her on the result. "I am glad, my dear," said he, "that the first year has been so smooth an one. I hope you find it an encouragement, and that you will not be dismayed if you should meet with a few rubs before long. We all meet with rubs, and you must expect your share."

"Certainly," replied Jane. "I am only surprised that we have done well so far. We owe it to your help, Sir. We could have done nothing without you."

"You can do some things without me, though, Jane. Remember you earned five guineas, without my knowing any thing of the matter. I cannot tell you how glad I am that Isabella is likely to prove a good help to you. She is a sweet girl, and will do us honour, when a few years have brought out her talents. But, my dear, she works very hard, and she is too young to work all day long. My wife is going to take the children to the sea, in July: if you will spare Isabella, a fortnight's run by the sea will bring more colour into her cheeks, and make her ready to begin school with new spirit."

Jane was beyond measure gratified by the indulgence offered to Isabella. She most thankfully accepted the kindness; and we cannot better close this part of our little history than by leaving our readers to imagine the actual happiness and hopeful anticipations of Jane, her sisters and brother, at the close of the first year, which had bound them together in those ties, the tenderness and strength of which only the fatherless can understand.

Chapter Three.

Few events worth recording happened during the next summer, autumn, and winter. The return of Mr Rathbone to London, which did not take place till the month of May, was the first remarkable circumstance which I have to relate. He asked Charles to dine at his house the Sunday after his arrival at home, and various and most kind were the enquiries he made about the whole family. He saw some specimens of Isabella's drawings, which pleased him much, and he expressed great satisfaction when he heard that Harriet was making excellent progress in music. He listened with benevolent interest when Charles spoke of Jane's exertions, of the mother's care which she bestowed on those who stood almost in the place of children to her. This was a subject on which Charles loved to speak, when he could find an auditor who could comprehend and would sympathise with his feelings. Such a listener he was aware that he now had, and his heart warmed more and more towards his benefactor with each moment in which he was allowed to dwell on a sister's praises. At length Mr Rathbone enquired how he who was so ready to make known the exertions of others, was himself going on in the world. "If you do not object to give me your confidence, Charles," said he, "I am as much interested in your concerns, as in your sisters."

Charles thanked him, and said there was but little to tell; and that little he communicated at once. He told Mr Rathbone the amount of his salary, and that of his expenditure. He told him how he was endeavouring to qualify himself for a higher situation, and what were the hopes which he ventured to indulge of affording his sisters some substantial assistance in time. At present he could do but little: the first year he had by great self-denial saved three pounds. This year he hoped to send Jane a five pound note on Midsummer Day, and in a year or two he had the prospect of a large salary.

Mr Rathbone questioned him closely as to his manner of living, and his plans of economy. Accustomed as he was to a very lavish expenditure, such economy as Charles's struck him with wonder; and he was surprised to find that so far from being despised by the young men among whom he was thrown, Charles was regarded with respect by all, with affection by some. He did not live in close, grudging solitude: he had lost none of the spirit of generous sociality which he brought with him to London, and preserved there, in spite of its chilling and counteracting influences. He was benevolent; he was generous. His purse he could in conscience open to none but his sisters; but his heart was open, his head was busy, and his hands were ready, whenever an opportunity of doing good occurred. Some of the young men with whom his situation connected him, gave entertainments to their friends, or made parties to go to places of public amusement. Charles could not do this; nor did he wish to offer, or accept, obligations of this kind; but all his companions readily acknowledged, from their own experience, that Charles had both the power and the inclination to do good. One had been ill, and had been nursed by Charles night and day, or as much of the day as he could call his own, so carefully and tenderly, that he owed his recovery in part, and the whole of what alleviation his disease admitted, to his benevolent care. Another had displeased Mr Gardiner, it was feared irremediably; and the young man would have gone to ruin, if Charles had not with indefatigable patience brought down his high and perverse spirit to the tone of apology and due humiliation; and, moreover, ventured to moderate his master's somewhat unreasonable anger. He got no thanks from either of them at the time: but he did not want thanks, and gained his end, which was, to see the youth re-established in his respectable situation. The hour of gratitude came at last, and Charles now knew that he might command every possible service from the youth whom he had obliged, and who was now proud to call him friend. He had rendered Mr Gardiner an essential service by informing him of the malpractices of some of the inferior people on the premises, which no one else had the courage to expose; and the widow with whom he lodged was obliged to him for her release from the oppression of a tyrannical landlord, who dared not trouble her, when he found that a spirited youth was her friend, who would not sit still and see her ill treated, while courage and activity could procure a remedy.

When we think that to these important services were added hourly kindnesses, most acceptable in the intercourses of social life; when we remember that where Charles was, there was cheerfulness, kindness, an open heart, a quick eye, and a ready hand to do good; we shall not wonder that he was beloved, though poor, and respected, though humble. Mr Rathbone was not, could not be, aware of all these things, but he heard Charles speak of the kindness that he experienced, and then it was easy to guess that it was earned by kindness shewn.

"I forget," said he, "how long it is exactly, since you came to London."

"Two years next month, Sir."

"And have you not seen your sisters in all that time?"

"No, Sir; nor have I any near prospect of seeing them. I do not venture to wish it, for fear of growing discontented. The girls are happy, and so am I; and we do not repine because we cannot reach an unattainable pleasure."

"I will try, Charles, whether it be unattainable. Two years of industry and self-denial deserve a reward. I will call on Mr Gardiner to-morrow, and beg for a fortnight's holiday for you. If I can obtain it, we will send you down to Exeter in a trice."

Charles's gratitude was inexpressible. In spite of his struggles, the tears started from his eyes. In a moment, his home and its beloved inmates rose up to his memory, and awakened his affections with an energy and vividness which he had never experienced before, in the deepest of the many reveries in which they had been presented to his fancy. Mr Rathbone understood his feelings, and so little doubted of being able to obtain this favour, that he tried to work up still more the ecstasy of hope which he had excited. "I have no doubt Mr Gardiner will spare you, Charles: you can be off by to-morrow night's coach."

But Charles had not so far forgotten common things in his joy, as to be unmindful that Jane would lose half the pleasure of his visit, if it was paid while she was engaged for the greater part of the day with her pupils. He knew that she was to have a fortnight's holiday at Midsummer, and he felt that it would be but justice to her, and the best economy of pleasure for himself, to defer his visit till that time, if possible. He did long, to be sure, to be off at once, and to take them by surprise, and he was afraid the intervening month would appear dreadfully long; but he felt that this was childish. He stated the case to Mr Rathbone, and begged that the request might be for the last week of June and the first of July.

He was much surprised to see a dark cloud pass over Mr Rathbone's brow while this explanation was being made: he could not believe it caused by any thing he had said, and therefore took no notice of it. The reply was, "It is not likely, *Sir*, that Mr Gardiner should let you choose your own time. I will mention it, however, and see what he says. I suppose you will not refuse to go now, if you cannot be spared afterwards?"

Poor Charles said what he thought best; but he was so astonished and grieved to have given offence, that his words did not come very readily. He tried in vain to forget Mr Rathbone's look and words; but, in spite of himself, he could not help endeavouring to account for what was unaccountable, and watching his benefactor's looks with intense anxiety.

The coldness passed off, and Mr Rathbone dismissed Charles with his usual kindness. Mrs Rathbone desired him not to trouble himself to call, if he should go the next night; but that, if his departure should be delayed for a month, she should wish to see him again. He would find her at home any morning before one o'clock.

The next day, about noon, Charles received a note, the contents of which were as follows.

> "Dear Charles,—
>
> "I have called on Mr Gardiner this morning, and he grants you leave of absence from the moment you read this till Wednesday fortnight; so that you have two clear weeks' holiday, and two days for going and coming. Mr G. can better spare you now than afterwards; so I hope you and your sister will find or make time for what you have to say to each other. I do not intend that this journey should break your five pound note. Let your sister have it, as you intended, and pay your expenses with that which is inclosed. I hope you will get a place in this night's coach, and that all will go well with you till we meet again.
>
> "Mrs Rathbone wishes you much pleasure, and requests you to take charge of the accompanying letter to Jane.
>
> "I am yours very sincerely,—
>
> "Francis Rathbone."

The inclosure was a ten pound note. Charles stood bewildered. The pressure of the time, however, made him collect his thoughts, and determine what was to be done. He first ran to the counting-house to thank Mr Gardiner briefly, but gratefully, for his indulgence. He next wrote a note, warmly expressive of his feelings, to Mr Rathbone: one of his friends in the warehouse engaged to leave it at the door that evening. Then Charles ran as fast as possible to secure a place in the coach. After some doubt and anxiety, he succeeded. He then bid his companions good-bye, and went to his lodgings to pack his little trunk and pay his bill. He then dined at a chop-house, and found that he had a clear hour left before it was time to depart. He did not hesitate how to employ it. There was a poor, a very poor family, who lived a little way from his lodgings, whose misery had caused Charles many a heart-ache. The mother was a daughter of the widow who was Charles's landlady, and it was through her that he knew any thing of them. Some trifling services he had been able to render these poor people, but with money he had not been able to assist them. Now, however, he felt himself so rich, from Mr Rathbone's bounty, that he thought he might indulge himself by bestowing a small present before his departure. He knew that one of the children was ill, and required better nourishment than their poverty could afford. He went to them, saw the child, sat with it while the mother went out to buy food with the half-crown which he had put into her hand, and left them with a light heart, followed by their blessings.

Who was ever happier than Charles at this moment? Whichever way his mind turned, it met only thoughts of peace and hope. The novelty of a journey, the freshness and beauty of the country in the brightness of a sweet evening in spring, the thought of two whole weeks of leisure, and of the sweet family intercourse which was to endear it, gratitude for benefits received, the sweet consciousness of benefits bestowed, all conspired to make him inexpressibly happy. His imagination represented to him all the possible situations in which the meeting with his family might take place. He was well enough acquainted with the house to fancy what the interior looked like; and he planned, in his fancy, where each of the family would be sitting, what each would be doing, and how each would express the astonishment and pleasure which his arrival must excite.

At length he fell asleep, and continued so, except for the occasional intervention of some pleasant dreamy thoughts, till the sunrise again roused him to the observation of the exquisite beauties of the fresh morning. The hours now passed less rapidly away, and he found his emotions becoming so tumultuous, that he tried to turn his thoughts upon indifferent subjects, and to enter into conversation with his fellow-passengers. As the day advanced, he became impatient of being shut in, so that he could catch only a confined view of the beautiful country through which he was passing, and he therefore took his seat on the roof of the coach. He sat next to a young man, who soon made acquaintance with him, and whom he found a very agreeable companion. His name Charles could not ascertain, but he found that he lived at Exeter, and it was interesting to them both to talk of persons and places with which both were familiar. In the afternoon, when they were still busy talking, and reckoning that four hours more would bring them to their journey's end, the coach stopped at a public-house by the road side, which the coachman entered, leaving a man at the horses' heads to take care of them. Some one called the man, and he left his charge, and the passengers did not for some moments perceive that he had done so, till something passed which caused the horses to start. Several men ran at once to catch the reins: this frightened the leaders yet more, and they set off at full gallop. Charles was sitting in front, and his companion, with much presence of mind, got over and seated himself on the box, and caught the reins. He attempted to pull in, but the screams of some of the passengers were enough of themselves to terrify any horses, and the young man's strength began to fail before they relaxed their speed at all. Still there was a wide road before them, with no apparent obstruction, and Charles, who tried to keep himself calm, hoped that the horses would soon be tired, and slacken their pace. He saw his companion's strength failing, and he leaned over and said, "Keep on one minute more and we shall do," when, most unfortunately, a waggon turned out of a field by the road side. The leaders turned sharp round, and upset the coach close by the hedge. Charles's fall was broken by the hedge, and he rose in a moment, with no other hurt than a few scratches from the briars; but such a dreadful scene of confusion met his view, that, though his first thought was to give help, he knew not where to turn. He looked for his companion, but could not see him, and hearing the most dismal screams from the inside of the coach, he entreated one or two persons, who were standing shaking their limbs, and apparently unhurt, to help him to get out the passengers. It was some time before they comprehended what he meant, and longer still before they could collect their senses sufficiently to be of any use. At length, however, Charles and another man climbed on the body of the coach, and pushed down the window. Two young ladies and a Quaker gentleman were inside. The latter said to Charles, "Lend me thy hand, for I am uppermost, and then we will rescue the others: there is not much harm done, I hope."

One of the ladies continued to scream so loud, that it was difficult to make her understand that she must use her own limbs in getting out. By main force, however, she was hauled through the window, and set on her feet. The Quaker gentleman said to her, "I recommend thee to be more quiet, if thou canst; if not, thou hadst better go a little out of the way, that we may know what we are doing. There is a stile yonder: sit there, and I will bring thy friend to thee."

The lady was able to comprehend this, and she accordingly moved away. There was more difficulty in rescuing her companion, who was really hurt: her arm was injured, and she was in great pain. She was quiet, however, and exerted what strength she had. Charles led her to some grass at a little distance: he hastily spread her cloak, and laid her down, and called her companion to her. When he reached the scene of disaster again, he was shocked to find that an outside passenger was killed. He was a dreadful object, and nothing was to be done, but to move him out of sight as quickly as possible. Still Charles looked round in vain for his companion; but when the noise had a little subsided, he thought he heard a faint groan from beneath the huge box-coat which was lying close by. Charles lifted it, and saw his companion lying with a large trunk upon one leg. He seemed in great agony, and unable to move. Charles called the Quaker gentleman. They gently lifted the trunk, and saw a sickening sight. The leg was dreadfully crushed. Charles for a moment turned away, but, ashamed of his weakness, he, with the Quaker's approbation, loosened the shawl which he wore round his neck, and wrapped it about the injured leg. They then raised the poor youth, and seated him on the trunk,

FRONTISPIECE.

Charles lifted up the coats and saw his companion lying with a large trunk upon one leg.

and tried to ascertain whether he had received any other injury. They could not detect any, but the sufferer was in so much pain, that they could not be sure. Charles beckoned to the waggoner, who was assisting the other passengers, and enquired whether there was any house nearer than the public-house which they had left, where the wounded passengers could be taken in for the present.

The man answered that there was none, and that they were three miles distant even from that.

Charles engaged him to convey the ladies and the young man in his waggon, which was filled with straw, and the people from the public-house having by this time reached the scene of disaster, the Quaker gentleman was able to accompany them. They therefore looked out their luggage, deposited the young man and the two ladies in the waggon, and returned to the public-house on foot. By the way they agreed what was further to be done. The Quaker thought the two ladies would be able to reach Exeter that night, and would prefer doing so to remaining in the inconvenient and crowded public-house. If the coach was able to proceed, so much the better; if not, a chaise could probably be procured. As for the young man, he must certainly remain; he was in no condition for travelling.

"I do not know," said Charles, "how you are circumstanced. We must not leave this poor youth; one of us must take charge of the ladies, and the other remain with him. Will you take your choice?"

"My wife is ill," replied the Quaker, "and I fear would be in terror, if she should hear of the accident, and not see me, even if I assured her of my welfare by my own hand. I should therefore prefer returning. But perhaps thou hast calls equally pressing?"

"No, I have not," replied Charles. "No one expects me: my family do not know that I am on my way to them: the matter therefore is decided."

"Not quite," said the Quaker. "The one who remains will have some painful scenes to go through. Thou art young: canst thou bear them?"

"I will *try* to bear them," replied Charles. "My heart aches for this young man, but it will be a comfort to be of service to him. We must learn his name, and you will call at his house as soon as you arrive, and inform his family; and some of them had better return in the chaise with a surgeon; for I suppose there is no medical advice to be had hereabouts."

"Probably not," replied the Quaker. "It is now nearly six: if we can procure a chaise without delay, in nine or ten hours hence his friends may be with him, and thou wilt be in part relieved from thy charge."

"He will be able to command himself," said Charles, "at least, if I may judge from his presence of mind at the time of the accident; and I shall therefore know better what to do, than if he were as unmanageable as that young lady."

"Her agony was so great," replied the Quaker, "that it would make one think that fear is, for the time, a greater evil than actual pain. Her sister (for I conclude they are sisters) was quiet enough; but it was beyond my power to stop her screams. Tell me how thy companion acted, for, being inside, I do not know."

Charles related how the youth had endeavoured to stop the horses.

"He indeed shewed self-command," said the good man, "and I am afraid he will have occasion to exercise all his resolution. I have no hope that that leg can be cured; but I hope his life is not in danger!"

"Can you," said Charles, "give me any directions respecting his treatment? Is there any thing to be done besides making him as easy as I can?"

"Nothing, that I am aware of," replied the Quaker. "I think thou wilt not have much need of thy purse for these few hours, or I would ask thee whether it is well filled?"

Charles thanked him, and assured him that no assistance of that kind was wanted.

By this time they had reached the public-house, and the young man was soon laid on a bed, in a decent though not very quiet apartment. On enquiry being made, it was found that no chaises were to be had there, but that a return chaise would probably pass very soon. The ladies were so incapable, one from pain, the other from terror, of judging what was best to be done, that the Quaker gentleman decided every thing for them. He directed the lady's arm to be bathed and hung in a sling, and advised them to accompany him in the chaise to Exeter, as soon as it should pass. Charles meanwhile was sitting by the bedside of the injured man, trying to ascertain the necessary particulars of his name, place of residence, etcetera. He was now able to speak, and said his name was Monteath, that his father and mother lived in — Street, Exeter, and that Mr Everett was the surgeon whom he wished to attend him. He said, "Are you going directly? must you leave me now?"

"I shall not leave you till your friends arrive," replied Charles. "Some of our fellow-passengers will carry our message to Exeter."

"Thank you! God bless you!" were the only words in answer. Presently he said, "Who are you? You have not told me your name."

Charles told his name.

"Forsyth!" exclaimed Mr Monteath; "surely you are the brother of Miss Forsyth, whom I have seen at Mr Everett's!"

"I am," said Charles.

"Then do not stay with me," said the youth; "your sister will be terrified when she hears of the accident."

Charles explained that his sisters did not expect him. He then enquired whether he did not suffer less than at first.

"Yes, I am rather easier," replied Monteath, "but still it is dreadful pain. However, I shall have worse to go through before I am better. I see what is before me: I do not wish to be blind to it."

"I am glad you are not blind to it," replied Charles. "You have strength of mind and self-command, and if you can keep up for a few hours, the worst will be over. Your present calmness assures me that you will keep up."

"I know not," replied Monteath. "Thoughts come crowding upon me faster than I can bear. This pain is not the worst: yet Oh! how it weakens me! I ought to feel, even at this moment, that all is right, that this suffering is for my good."

"It is," said Charles; "and it is this thought which has comforted me for you. In a few hours you will, I trust, be at ease, and, after that, all will come easy to you. In the mean time, think whose hand has brought this evil upon you, and remember that he is pitying your pain. He also gives strength and courage to those who ask for them."

"I will seek for them," replied Monteath. "Leave me for a while: I will try to compose my mind, and strengthen myself for these hours of pain."

Charles drew the curtains round the bed, and sat down in the window-seat. He did feel sick at heart. His head throbbed, and his heart beat thick, when he thought of the agony he had witnessed, of what was yet to be undergone by his companion, and of the dreadful disclosure which must be made to the father and mother, who were now probably counting the minutes as they flew, in the hope of a joyous meeting with their son. By degrees, he became aware that he was looking only at the dark side of the picture. He reproached himself for overlooking the mercies which had attended this dispensation. His own preservation, that of many besides, that only one life was lost among so many, that the suffering had fallen upon those who were apparently the best able to bear it; and he was not forgetful that the warning which was afforded them all of the uncertainty of life, and health, and peace, was of itself a great mercy. He now remarked the sun disappearing behind the hills, and remembered how he had watched it declining in the heavens, with the confident expectation that the hours of succeeding darkness would be spent in the home of his sisters; that, before the sun should rise again, he would have embraced them, have looked on their faces, and heard their voices, and exchanged affectionate greetings with them. Now the night was to be passed beside the bed of pain, and the sunrise would find him, probably, exhausted and spiritless, and still far from those he loved. "What a little way can we see!" thought Charles: "how uncertain should we ever feel of the future! how prepared for whatever may happen! how grateful for every exemption from suffering! I am not happy now; I cannot be happy while one is near me who is suffering severely: but let me be grateful: let me remember my preservation from personal injury, and let me trust that those who suffer will find strength and comfort from Him who has blessed and preserved me."

While these thoughts passed through his mind, tears coursed each other down his cheeks. He did not check them, for he found relief from these quiet tears. He was, meantime, not forgetful of his charge: he listened to his breathing; it was, at first, loud and irregular, as of one in pain, and now and then a deep sob could be heard. Still Charles sat quiet, for he judged rightly that Monteath would be better able to compose himself, if left undisturbed. By degrees, his breathing became more regular, and all was so quiet, that Charles hoped he was at ease, if not asleep. Meanwhile it was becoming dark, and as night advanced, the public-house was more quiet, and Charles entertained the hope that his friend might be strengthened for his approaching suffering, by a few hours of repose. When the last tinge of brightness had faded from the clouds, and was succeeded by total darkness, Charles still remained in the window-seat: he would not procure a light for fear of noise; and he continued to look out, though nothing was to be seen, but a servant occasionally crossing the yard with a lantern, which cast a dim gleam through the room. The ticking of his watch was the only sound that he heard. It was too dark to see what time it was, but when he imagined he had been sitting about two hours, the loud ringing of a bell broke the silence, and disturbed poor Monteath, who had really been asleep. He attempted to move, but the attempt extorted a deep groan. Charles sprang to the bedside, and spoke to him. "You are in pain again," said he, "but you have been easier, and will be so again soon."

Monteath could not answer him.

Charles rang for a light. It was brought, and Monteath asked what o'clock it was. It was near eleven. "No more!" said he, and he enquired how soon his father and mother could be with him. Charles thought in four or five hours, and he told his friend that if he would be prevailed on to take a little refreshment, he thought he might sleep again.

"O, no, do not ask me to move," replied Monteath.

"You need not move," replied Charles. "I will give it you, while you lie still: but indeed you need it."

"I will," said Monteath. "But have you been beside me all this time, without any refreshment? You must be quite exhausted. Pray go down and have some supper: I shall not want you just now: why did you not leave me?"

Charles, though little inclined to eat, consented to have some supper brought up, but he would not leave his friend. He asked Monteath if he had not enjoyed his repose.

"It was a great rest," was the reply; "but I believe I have had my poor mother in my mind almost all the time. I am afraid she is more unhappy than I am at this moment."

"But when she hears that you have slept, and when she sees you able to speak, and even to comfort her, as I think you will, she will be relieved."

"They will have Mr Everett with them," said Monteath, "and he is a kind and judicious friend. It is he who must free me from this pain," added he. "I hope I shall not hate him for the office, as I have heard that some people hate their surgeons, in spite of themselves."

"No fear of that," said Charles.

"I hope they will not delay it," said Monteath. "I would fain hope that in twelve hours, it will be over. I almost think it cannot be worse than what I suffered when I was lying on the road, before you found me."

"Probably not so bad, and most probably much sooner over. Some people would think me wrong in letting you speak of this, but I think it will do you no harm. You would think about it at all events, and it makes anticipated evils less, to talk rationally about them."

"You are right," said Monteath. "I have been looking steadily at the whole matter, and I want to ask you one thing. Mr Everett will perhaps bring no assistant. If he does not, will you, can you, stand by, and prevent my father from being present? I know he will insist on it, if no friend is at hand but Mr Everett."

"I can, and I certainly will," replied Charles. "I have never attempted any thing of the kind, but I think I can make my resolution equal to the occasion. If I can be of use, I shall not think of myself."

"Thank you, thank you," replied Monteath. "Things might have been worse with me yet. There might have been no one who would have had compassion on me, no friend who would have comforted me as you are doing."

"I can do little," said Charles. "There is a better friend with you, who can yield support when earthly friends are far away, or too feeble to give comfort. I hope you feel this."

"I do now, more than ever in my life before. Just now, I was in too much pain to think of any thing: but I am easy enough to think, and speak, and listen, at present. Have you a Bible with you?"

Charles instantly produced his Bible, and asked his friend what he should read.

"The forty-second and forty-third Psalms first," said Monteath.

Charles read them, and afterwards chose a chapter in the New Testament, and with pleasure he perceived that Monteath appeared more and more tranquil, and in a little time he enjoyed the repose which his exhausted frame required.

He slept till three o'clock, and was then too anxious for the arrival of his father and mother to rest again. Charles attempted to interest him in conversation, and he was interested; but he started at every little noise, and to say the truth, Charles was little less nervous than himself. At length, almost before they could reasonably expect it, they distinctly heard a chaise drive up.

"O, go, go!" cried Monteath. "Go and bring them to me!"

"Not yet," said Charles, firmly. "I will go to them, but they must not see you till I can tell them that you are more calm. Compose yourself, and remember that the best comfort you can give them is to see you tranquil. I will tell them that you have slept, and in a few minutes you shall see them; in the mean time compose yourself."

Charles went down stairs, and the first meeting with Mr and Mrs Monteath was very painful. He was glad, however, to give them some comfort, and he spoke as cheerfully as he could of the night which his friend had passed. Presently he conducted them to their son's chamber, and left them at the door. Mr Everett enquired the particulars of the accident, and the extent of the injury, as far as Charles could judge of it. He shook his head, when he had heard the particulars, and said he feared there was no help for it, but that the leg must be amputated.

"Thinking this would be necessary," he said, "I brought an assistant with me; and I am glad I did, for delay would be dangerous; and I suppose there is no surgeon near. Is your friend prepared for it?"

"Perfectly," replied Charles: "and he thinks the sooner it is done, the better. How soon will it be, Sir?"

"Directly, if it has to be done," replied Mr Everett, "but you know I have not seen him yet, and therefore cannot be sure that it will be necessary."

Mr and Mrs Monteath came down presently, and told Mr Everett that their son wished to see him. Before he went, he told them that he should recommend their trying to get some rest.

"Now that your son has seen you, he will sleep again," said he, "and I wish to remain alone with him for two or three hours. He will not rest if you are beside him, so you must trust him with me, and our young friend will bring you news of him from time to time."

The father and mother were obliged to consent: they retired, and Charles took his station in the next room to his friend. In a few minutes Mr Everett's assistant came out of the chamber, and soon after returned with a servant, and there were signs of preparation which were sickening to poor Charles. He made a great effort to forget himself, however, and gently opening the chamber door, asked if he could be of use.

"You can, Sir, if you think yourself able," replied Mr Everett. "I believe we may trust you, for you are aware of the importance of self-command just now. I advise you to take a glass of wine, and then go and speak to your friend, and we will call you when we want you."

Charles did so.

"Your mother has gone to lie down," he whispered; "by the time she wakes, we shall have comfort to give her, and you will be better able to see her."

Monteath pressed his hand. "I am better than I was," said he; "stronger in mind, too. I do believe I dreaded seeing my mother more than any thing else."

Mr Everett now approached the bed, and in a short time, which, however, appeared to Charles as if it never would be over, the painful thing was done, and Monteath was in bed again. Charles remained beside him, and in an hour the patient was once more in a sound sleep. Mr Everett went then to tell his father and mother what had been done. They were dreadfully agitated at first, but the sight of their son in deep repose calmed them, and every thing was soon so comfortably arranged, that Charles thought his assistance was no longer needed. He went to bed, rested till the middle of the day, and in the afternoon proceeded with Mr Everett to Exeter, the assistant being left behind with the patient, and Mr Everett promising to return the next day but one. Monteath did not | know how to express his gratitude, and his parents' acknowledgments were painful to Charles, who felt that in common humanity he could not have done less than he had done. They however thought differently, and were grateful, not only for what he had done, but for the manner of doing it; and felt very sure, that, painful as that night had been to Charles, every recollection of it would bring pleasure as long as he lived. He promised his friend that he would not return to London without seeing him, and then set off, wondering when he thought that his acquaintance with Monteath had been of only twenty-four hours' standing, and that, in that time, he had been called on to perform more painful offices of kindness, than generally devolve upon intimate friends during a connexion of many years.

"At this hour yesterday," thought Charles, "we met for the first time, and now we are perhaps friends for life. It has been proved, by a fiery trial, that Monteath has many virtues. I know, beyond a doubt, that he is religious, that he is attached to his family, that he is considerate to others, that he is courageous and patient. This is a great deal to have learned in twenty-four hours. If I were to consider myself alone, I might rejoice in this accident. I have gained a valuable friend, and received a lesson which I shall never forget, at the expense of only a few hours of salutary pain. But I am the last person to be considered. Better fruits even than these may spring from this calamity, to those who have at present suffered more from it."

The journey with Mr Everett was cheerful and pleasant. Charles had now the opportunity of learning a great deal about his sister Jane; and all that he heard gave him pleasure. His home and its inmates had been forgotten for some hours, but now he began again to anticipate the pleasures of meeting, though with much less confidence than before. At first he felt almost sure that something would yet happen to delay their meeting; but when they were within five miles of the city, he began to recognise some well-known object at every step, and to feel a quieter hope that at length he should reach his journey's end in peace. He started up at the first sight of the Cathedral towers, and gazed at them till he actually passed them. Then he looked for familiar faces, and as the chaise turned the corner into the market-place, a boy looked up from the foot pavement, who, tall as he was, could, Charles was sure, be no other than Alfred. "It *is* Alfred," said Mr Everett, "going home to tea, I guess. You will find them just sitting down to tea, the lessons all learned, the business all done, and nothing to do but to talk and listen."

The chaise stopped, and Charles was soon on his way home, with his little trunk under his arm. When Hannah answered his knock, she knew him instantly, and started back, calling, "Miss Jane, Miss Jane!"

Miss Jane rose from the tea-table, and she and Charles met at the parlour door. "Charles! my dear, dear Charles! What can have brought you? What are you here for?"

"I am come to see you, my dearest; and you, and you," added he, turning to the others, as they pressed round him. "I am come for a whole fortnight. Now, dearest, I have taken you too much by surprise," for Jane's tears flowed fast. "Come, come, compose yourself. Look up, and smile at me."

Jane hung on his shoulder. He led her to a chair, Isabella seated herself on the other side, and Harriet sprung on his knee. "I should not have startled you so," said Charles, "but I had no time to write, and give you notice. I did not know myself, till a few hours before I left town, that I was coming."

"But *how* did you come?" asked Isabella. "This is not the time when any of the coaches arrive."

"My dear, I must explain all that by and by: there is a long and sad story connected with that."

"I am glad we knew nothing about your coming," said Alfred; "for the London coach was overturned yesterday, and we should have been afraid that you were in it."

"It *was* overturned, and there was a man killed," said Charles; but he said no more about it, for he did not feel inclined to enter at once upon that sad subject.

"I am afraid, Jane, I am not come at the pleasantest time for you: your mornings are, I suppose, fully engaged, but we must make long evenings."

"And here is one to begin with," said Jane. "We have you all to ourselves for this evening at least. But how very tired you look! Are you quite well?"

"Perfectly," replied Charles, "I am only tired."

"Come and have some tea," said Isabella. "Let me make tea to-night, Jane, and do you sit beside Charles."

So the happy party gathered round the table, and it would be in vain for us to attempt to follow them through the variety of subjects which they touched upon, or to record half that was said. After tea, Charles went into the kitchen to speak to Hannah, and to delight her by his affectionate remembrance. Then Jane and Harriet had to settle the important affair of where Alfred was to sleep. He was to give up his bed to Charles, and a little bed was made up for him, in a corner of the same room. He declared that he would sleep on the floor rather than that Charles should seek a lodging out of the house.

Late in the evening a note arrived from Mrs Everett: an unusually gracious one for her. It said that, as Miss Forsyth and her brother had not met for so long, Mrs Everett would be sorry to keep them asunder, for the few first days of his stay, especially as Mr C. Forsyth must require cheering and relaxation, after the melancholy circumstances of his journey. Mrs Everett therefore would not require Miss Forsyth to resume her daily charge till the next Monday, and in the mean time wished her much enjoyment of her brother's society.

"How very kind!" exclaimed Jane.

"How perfectly delightful!" said Charles.

"But how should Mrs Everett know that you are here, Charles?" said Isabella. "News must fly faster than I thought it did, if any body has told her that you are come."

"I will explain it all in the morning," said Charles, "it is too long a story to tell now."

"I wish," said Harriet, "*we* had a holiday till Monday. If the news has got to Mrs Everett's, it might as well spread a little further: just as far as Mrs —'s ears."

"I should like a holiday very well," said Isabella, "but Charles and Jane had rather be alone, I suppose; and I had rather they should, for part of the time."

Charles thanked her by a kiss, for her consideration.

It was with a deep feeling of gratitude and delight that he this evening joined in family worship for the first time for two years. Jane read the Psalm and chapter with a somewhat tremulous voice this evening, and sweet and touching was that voice to her brother's ear, and he deeply felt the words of thanksgiving which were uttered by it. "*Bless the Lord,*

O my soul; and all that is within me, bless his holy name. Bless the Lord, O my soul, and forget not all his benefits: who forgiveth all thine iniquities; who healeth all thy diseases; who redeemeth thy life from destruction; who crowneth thee with loving-kindness and tender mercies."

What words could be so apt as these to express thankfulness for the preservation of life, and for the subsequent bestowment of the sweetest blessings which endear it to the pure and uncorrupted heart? Sweet was it also to join with his best friends in a prayer for the continuance of these mercies, and for the blessing of their Giver upon their enjoyment. The weight of sadness which had still pressed upon Charles's mind, and which nothing else had availed to lighten, was now removed by the exercise of prayer, and with a light as well as thankful heart he retired to rest. He awoke from refreshing sleep when Alfred rose the next morning; and when they were assembled at breakfast, he told his promised tale of the extraordinary events of his journey. The name of Monteath was not unknown to the Forsyths, and Jane had seen this very youth at the Everetts' more than once, and knew that he was a great favourite in their family. Charles expressed his intention of calling on his Quaker friend, if he could find him, and also at Mr Monteath's house, to learn if any further account of his friend had arrived. Mr Barker also was to be seen, and plans were to be laid for the employment of the precious days of Charles's stay. Before these were half arranged, it was time for the younger ones to be off to school; and when the brother and sister found themselves really alone, Charles produced Mrs Rathbone's letter, which he rightly judged must be partly on business. It was indeed of considerable importance.

Mrs Rathbone wrote in her husband's name, as well as her own. She said that Jane had probably heard through Mr Barker that they hoped to be of use to Alfred whenever it should be time to think of placing him out: that it was time the boy should have some idea of his future destination, and that his family should know what to look forward to. She went on to say,—

> "Mr Rathbone has influence in India, and if Alfred's talents are what we understand them to be, there can be no doubt of his distinguishing himself in the Company's service, and of procuring solid advantages to his family. Our views for him are these. We shall take the charge of his education at the Company's military schools, where he will be qualified for being a military engineer in the forces in India. In five years he will be sent out, and then he

will only have to exert himself to get forward, to distinguish himself, and probably to enrich his family, for there are perhaps no other means by which wealth can be so easily acquired. It appears to us that there is no other way in which we can so effectually assist you as this; and few things can give us more pleasure than the anticipation of the time when you will be easy and prosperous, and look back on your present labours and cares as on a long past dream. Alfred will rejoice to promote the prosperity of that kind sister who devoted herself to his welfare when he was too young to repay her cares, and that sister will rejoice in the honour and wealth which his well directed exertions will be the means of conferring on his family.

"As you are all bound together by even closer ties of affection than usually unite those of the same family, it is natural that you should grieve at the prospect of a separation from Alfred of many years. These separations are certainly sad things; but I have too good an opinion of your sense and your self-command to suppose that you will set the gratification of even your dearest and most cherished feelings against the solid interests of the family who depend upon you, and of whom you are the head. This is the only objection to our plan which we anticipate from you, unless it be the consideration of health. But this is a thing so entirely uncertain, so many die at home, and so many sustain the trial of a foreign climate, and live to old age in it, that we cannot foresee and calculate, and therefore should not suffer our plans to be deranged by too much regard to this consideration, but should trust, that, whether at home or abroad, all will be well with those whom we love. You will let us know soon what you think of our plan, and you will make up your mind to part with Alfred at the end of a year from next Midsummer. In the mean time, he had better continue at the school where he now is, and the only direction we have to give is, that he will continue to devote his attention to mathematics. If tolerably advanced in this branch of study, he will set out with the more advantage in his new studies next year.

"We should like to see Alfred, and form our own judgment of him; and for this purpose, and also to afford him some pleasure, we hope you will not object to his spending a fortnight with us in the approaching holidays. Charles will let us know when to expect him, and we will make him as happy as we can. We have chosen the present opportunity of developing our plan to you, as we thought you would like to have Charles by your side to talk to concerning it. Wishing you much enjoyment together, and assuring you of our interest in all your concerns, I am, my dear young friend,—

"Most truly yours,—

"Sarah Rathbone."

Charles and Jane looked at each other when they had finished reading this letter. "Well, Jane," said Charles, "what is your opinion of it?"

"O, Charles, I do not at all like it. But we cannot judge till we have thought about it."

"Let us think about it then," said Charles.—"In the first place, could you part with Alfred for many years, if you were thoroughly convinced that it would be for his good and ours?"

"I could, I hope, *if* I were convinced of that. But what good could counterbalance all the evils of such a separation to him and us?"

"Let us consider the good first, Jane, and then we will weigh the evil against it. This is not a new idea to me; I had some suspicion of Mr Rathbone's plans, and so I have thought a little about the matter. If Alfred goes, we may have it in our power to repay our friends here the obligations we are under to them now; (I mean, of course, the pecuniary part of the obligation;) and we may be able to place Isabella and Harriet in a situation in society where their talents and virtues may be exercised with as much benefit to others, and without such painful labour and care as will probably be their lot, if, as we have hitherto expected, they have to work for their own subsistence. Are not these real, solid advantages?"

"I believe they are," replied Jane. "And you too—"

"O, I am out of the question just now, and so are you, Jane. We must now forget ourselves, and even each other, if we mean to decide coolly for the good of those who depend on us. Are there any other advantages? Is honour, fame, or whatever else we call it, a good?"

"What kind of honour will it be?" asked Jane. "The honour of bravery, I suppose—a soldier's glory."

"More than that," said Charles. "He may have the reputation of talent, of industry, and of general honourable principle."

"This kind of reputation is valuable in many respects," said Jane; "but it may be had at home as well as in India, better perhaps: for I do not know how to reconcile the rapid acquisition of wealth with honourable principle."

"Nor I," said Charles. "Well, do you reckon this honour an advantage?"

"I think not," said Jane. "I do not desire a mere soldier's glory for any one I love, since it is bought by violence, and must therefore harden the heart: and honour of a better kind may be had, as far as it is desirable, at home."

"I quite agree with you," said Charles. "Then again, the increase of knowledge, and enlargement of mind, which is obtained by travelling, and intercourse with foreign nations, is, in my opinion, a real advantage, though Mrs Rathbone does not mention it. We are not considering how it is counterbalanced; but is it not in itself a good?"

"It is," said Jane; "and now I fancy we have come to the end of the list. For power, influence, high connexions, the ability to exercise beneficence, all come under the heads of wealth and honour: and as to the benefit to Alfred of exerting himself for his family, that also may be had at home, and may be all the more beneficial for the wealth not being got so easily as in India. But *health* is the grand objection. I do wonder at the way in which Mrs Rathbone speaks of this. She speaks of many who die in England as well as in India: but who does not know the difference in the proportions? And she speaks of *trust* too, as if foresight and precaution were inconsistent with it."

"And of those who live," said Charles, "how few, if any, return in health! Mr Rathbone himself is rich: but who would take his riches in exchange for the health he has sacrificed?"

"Have we any right to consent to such a probable sacrifice for Alfred?" said Jane.

"Certainly not, in my opinion," said Charles. "But there is another question of greater importance still—Alfred's moral welfare. His early separation from his family would be a sad thing; but not half so fearful as the risk of sending him into the society of the dissolute, or, at best, the careless, where his duty will lie in scenes of bloodshed and devastation, where his employment will be to contrive and execute plans for spreading ruin and wasting life. Can we devote him to an employment like this? Some may represent the matter in a different light, and say that he is promoting the prosperity of his country and the extension of commerce by his services. But I say, let him, if he serves his country, serve it by innocent means; by means reconcileable to the law of God, and to the duty which man owes to man: let him do this, even if he live and die in hardship and poverty, rather than corrupt his mind, and harden his heart, and become such a one as we could not love, though he were to make himself and us as rich and powerful as the most worldly could desire."

"Oh, Charles, if this is all true, who could doubt for a moment? How could Mr Rathbone think of such a plan for a moment?"

"Different people," said Charles, "see things in a different light. Mr Rathbone has not experienced these dangers, because he has made his fortune by commerce, not by war. Besides, I must think Mr Rathbone a very rare instance of the power of principle against temptation. There are few indeed who spend their Indian wealth so generously for others, though every one who goes out with any principle to direct him, hopes that *he* shall be able to hold a straight course, though almost all others have gone astray. I could not, neither, I am sure, could you, encourage this confidence with respect to Alfred. If he were to be separated from us for five years before he left England, and were to have no prospect of seeing us again for twenty or thirty years, how weak would be the family ties, and how easily chilled the family affection on which we should wish to depend as a safeguard to higher principles! And as to those higher principles, *we* could have little influence in forming or strengthening them: we must, at the end of one other year, commit them to the care of strangers. How little knowledge we could have of them; how little confidence that they could be firm enough to resist the attacks of temptations, renewed from day to day, under which the strong have sunk, and before which the fortified have given way."

"But Charles, my dear Charles, is this all true? Are you sure there is no mistake? If but one hundredth part were true, I would not hesitate for a moment."

"Ask those who know, dear Jane: let us ask Mr Barker. Let us tell our thoughts to Mr Rathbone himself. This is too important a matter to be decided on our own judgments, without further knowledge; but Mr Barker's knowledge of the fate of many youths who have been sent out to India, will, I believe, lead him to encourage us in declining Mr

Rathbone's offer. Whatever we may think of the offer itself, Jane, we must not forget the generosity which has been shewn in making it."

"Certainly," said Jane, "it will be very difficult to express our sense of such kindness; and more so still to decline it: but I hope they will understand and even approve our feeling about it."

The brother and sister then talked over other circumstances connected with their affairs. Charles asked whether any new plan was in view for the girls to earn a little more money. Jane smiled, and said that Isabella had not been idle, but that what she had attempted was yet unfinished, and that if Charles had not visited them, he would have known nothing of the matter till the work was completed. The thing was this: a French lady who had been staying at Mr Everett's in the autumn, had shewn Jane an elegant little French work on plants. A variety of flowers were arranged according to various peculiarities, which had caused them to be adopted as emblems, some of royalty, others of natural or moral qualities, etcetera. There were plates of many of the flowers, some well executed, others very indifferently. It struck Jane at once that Isabella might translate this work, and she borrowed it of the French lady, that they might examine it at home. They thought, on close examination, that the work might be improved in the translation: that various floral emblems might be added, and that drawings, very superior to the plates of the work, might increase its value. When Jane returned the book, she asked its owner whether it had been translated into English. The reply was, that the original work had only been published a few weeks, and could not yet be well known in England. This determined Isabella at once to make the trial. The drawings were the most important and the most difficult part; but by the interest and assistance of a few friends, Isabella obtained access to some excellent botanical works and plates. Many, indeed most of the flowers, she was able to draw from nature during the eight months that the work was in progress; and where the flowers were so rare as to be out of her reach altogether, there was nothing to be done but to copy from the plates of the original work. With the translation she took great pains, and here Jane helped her. Jane had an excellent and well-cultivated taste, and she was therefore well fitted to judge of style, and she assisted Isabella to re-write and polish her translation, till no foreign idiom could be detected, and till there was no trace of the stiffness or poverty which characterises most versions from the French. When this was done, Jane, who wrote a much better hand than Isabella, transcribed it, by degrees, as the drawings were finished, one by one, so that the work was complete as far as it went. At this time, only four drawings and about twelve pages of copying remained to be done, and then it was to try its fate in the hands of a London bookseller.

Charles was delighted with the plan, as Jane described it; but she would not let him see the work till Isabella was present. She said that if it did not answer she should be quite grieved, for that it had been the object of chief interest to Isabella for many months, and she had been unwearied in her application to it during all her leisure hours in that time. They could form no idea of the sum it ought to bring them; but Jane said she would not take less than ten guineas, and she hoped for more. Charles shook his head, and was afraid she expected too much; but he promised to take charge of it when he returned, if it could be finished by that time, and to do all in his power to dispose of it advantageously. He then enquired whether the five guineas which they had already earned remained untouched; and on being told that it was to lie by till they were rich enough to purchase a piano, or till some unforeseen emergency should call it into use, he presented his own five pound note to Jane to add to the little fund.

Jane was most unwilling to receive the fruits of his labour and self-denial; but she knew that he spoke the truth when he said that no other use to which he could apply it would give him half so much pleasure. It gave him pleasure, he said, to think that they had a little sum of their own to go to, instead of having to apply to their friends in case of sickness, family mourning, or any other incidental expense likely to occur in a family consisting of several members, and widely, though distantly, connected with many more. "It is not being over-prudent, Jane; it is not being worldly-minded, I hope, to think in this way, is it?"

"I think not," replied Jane. "I am often afraid of becoming so, I assure you, and I try to keep this fear in mind from day to day. At present, however, we have been led on so easily, our path has been so smoothed for us, that it seems hardly possible that we should be unmindful *who* it is that has disposed all things for us. *Now* I am reminded, day by day, how grateful I ought to be: if I become worldly, it will more probably be when I have greater labours and anxieties to undergo. If we can meet in this way, dear Charles, from time to time, it will be as strong a safeguard against worldliness as we can have."

In the course of the morning Charles called on his Quaker travelling companion, and gave him an account of the night which he had passed with poor Monteath, and of the circumstances under which he had left his charge. The excellent man was much interested, and said he wished that he could himself have remained, and saved Charles the pain of these anxious hours.

"My wife," said he, "was saved much fear by my speedy arrival, I hope thy friends had no fear for thee?"

"My sisters," replied Charles, "were not aware of my journey, as it fortunately happened."

"And thy father and mother: hadst thou not a father and mother to await thy arrival?"

Charles shortly explained his family circumstances.

"Thy sister must have a strong mind, like thine, to conduct a household, and to employ herself in another responsible situation also; considering that she is yet young. Thou wilt come again?" said he, seeing that Charles was preparing to depart, "thou wilt come again? Uncommon circumstances have made us acquainted, and I should be unwilling to discontinue our acquaintance, as it may be pleasant to both of us."

Charles promised to call again.

"My wife, as I told thee, is ill," said Mr Franklin, (for that was his name,) "and therefore cannot go to see thy sister; but if thou wilt take thy tea with us to-morrow, and if thy sister will disregard ceremony, and come with thee, we shall be glad."

Charles accepted the invitation with great pleasure, as he thought that this respectable family might prove pleasant and valuable friends to Jane.

He next called on Mr Barker, who was not a little astonished at the sight of him. Charles told him that Jane and he were anxious to have his advice on the important subject of Mrs Rathbone's letter. Mr Barker promised to devote the first leisure time he had to them. Charles next called at Mr Monteath's door, to enquire concerning his friend; but no account had arrived, or was expected before the evening.

When the messenger arrived, he brought a favourable report. The patient was easy, and all was going on right. He sent, by his mother's letter, an affectionate message to Charles, and said, he hoped by the time his father returned to Exeter to be able to write a note himself to his friend.

Mr Barker called in the evening to see Mrs Rathbone's letter respecting Alfred, and to consult with Jane and her brother on the subject. They plainly told him their feelings upon it, their dislike to the military profession, especially.

Mr Barker was silent, and looked thoughtful.

"Are we wrong, Sir?" asked Charles. "Have we got high-flown or mistaken notions about this? or is it presumptuous in us, who are so poor, and under great obligations, to affect a choice for our brother?"

"No, my dear boy; none of these. I was silent because I was thinking of a sad story, and wondering whether I should tell it you. Have you quite made up your minds to reject Mr Rathbone's offer?"

"That depends on your opinion," said Jane. "If you shew us that Charles's ideas of the hazard and probable misery of such a destination, are mistaken, we must deliberate further: but if what I have heard be true, I would as soon see Alfred in his coffin as incur so fearful a responsibility."

"I think what Charles has said is all true: but, my dears, you must prepare yourselves for something which will be to you very terrible."

"Mr Rathbone's displeasure," said Charles. "I feared that: but grateful as we are and ought to be for his most disinterested generosity to us, we ought to look on his gifts as curses, if they take from us the liberty of unbiassed choice, where the moral welfare of a brother is in question."

"Say so in your reply to him, Charles."

"But it may be," said Jane, "that he will not be displeased. We take for granted much too readily, I think, that he will misunderstand us."

"Mr Rathbone's temper is peculiar," replied Mr Barker. "A somewhat haughty spirit was rendered imperious by the power and rank he possessed in India. Considering this, it is wonderful that he should retain so generous a disposition as his is; but every one knows, and Charles himself must have observed, that he cannot bear to be opposed, especially in any scheme of benevolence."

Jane sighed. "At any rate," said she, "he cannot prevent our being grateful for what he has done, and for his present kind intentions. It is hard to be obliged to estrange such a friend, but it would be harder still to devote Alfred to danger, and to temptations stronger than we dare encounter ourselves."

"The estrangement will not be your work, but his own, Jane: that is, if you write such a letter as I expect you will. Do not let your fear of offending cramp your expression. Speak your gratitude freely, and also your resolution of independence. Write as freely as you have been speaking to me."

"May I shew you my letter, Sir, and have your opinion of it?" asked Jane.

"By all means," replied Mr Barker, "and the sooner it is done the better."

"We have been saved much pain," said Charles, "by your entire agreement with us. I thought you would think as we did; but yet it is generally believed a very fine thing to get a young man out to India."

"It is," said Mr Barker: "and in my young days a brother of my own was sacrificed to this mistaken belief. So you will not wonder that I view the matter in the same light as you do. It is a very common story. He left home as good and promising a youth as could be, but too young. Fine visions of wealth and grandeur floated before him: poor fellow! he desired them more for his family than for himself when he set out on his career; but his affections gradually cooled as time rolled on, and the prospect of seeing his home again was still very distant. As he thought less of his family he thought more of himself, and gave more and more into habits of self-indulgence. He got money very fast, and occasionally sent some home, but squandered much more on his own pleasures. Then, as might be expected, his health failed: he dragged on a miserable existence for many months, till an attack of illness, which would formerly have been overcome in two days' time, carried him off, a feeble and unresisting prey. He was thought to have left a large property, but it could never be got at; and I have heard my poor father say that he was glad we never had a farthing of it, for it would have seemed to him the price of blood. It was a mistake, however, and only a mistake; for his welfare was the object of his parents: but it was a mistake whose consequences weighed them down with sorrow to their dying days."

After Mr Barker was gone, this little family gathered together to close the day with an hour of pleasant intercourse. Isabella's work was produced, and extremely did Charles admire it. "Will it bring her ten guineas?" asked Jane.

"Twenty, or nothing," said Charles. "Only, I am no judge of these things. You must get it done for me to take back with me, Isabella."

Isabella thought it was impossible she could have earned twenty guineas so easily. Not very easily, Charles thought: the leisure hours of eight months had been spent upon this, and great efforts of perseverance and resolution had been required. Add to this, the uncertainty and delay and hazard which she yet had to encounter, and he thought that twenty guineas was no more than a sufficient recompense. He told her that all would not be over when the work was finished, but that she might have to wait many months before she knew its fate, and it was even very possible that it might remain on her hands. Isabella, however, had made up her mind to be patient and to hope for the best.

When they separated for the night, Jane whispered to her brother,— "Yes, we will keep together and be happy. Better is poverty in this house, than wealth in India." Charles kissed her in sign of agreement.

The next morning Jane sat down to write her letter, with her brother by her side. He approved the simple account which she gave of their feelings and opinions upon the important matter, and made her add, that she and her brother had the sanction of Mr Barker's experienced judgment. Mr Barker had given her permission to say this, and when Charles shewed him the letter, he approved the whole of it, and it was therefore sealed and dispatched. Jane endeavoured to forget her fears about the answer, and determined to bear it patiently, whatever it might be, knowing that she had acted to the best of her judgment. During the walk which she afterwards took with her brother she forget this subject and every other, for he told her over again, and more completely, the history of the night he had passed with poor Monteath. On their return home they made enquiry again at Mr Monteath's door, and heard that the young man was going on so well, that his father would return to Exeter in two days.

Charles heard from Mr Franklin that evening some further particulars respecting Monteath's family, and respecting himself. He was in business with his father, and had lately become a partner. They were not supposed to be rich, but were universally esteemed for their integrity. There were several sisters, one older, and the rest younger than their brother; but he was the only brother, and the pride and delight of the family. The good Quaker was evidently affected when he spoke of the sorrow which this sad accident had brought among them, and yet more when he spoke of an attachment which was supposed to exist between Monteath and a young lady who was at present staying with his sisters. Mr Franklin had been at the house that morning, and the young ladies had expressed in strong terms their gratitude to Charles, and the desire they had to see this friend of their brother. When their father returned they hoped to be able to shew that they were not insensible and ungrateful. Mr Franklin told them that Charles was to be at his house that evening, and he promised to take him to call, if he would be induced to go. Charles only thought himself too much honoured for what he believed any one of common humanity would have done in his circumstances, and he accordingly left Jane with Mrs Franklin, and accompanied his friend to Mr Monteath's. He saw the two eldest ladies, but not their friend, which he was glad of, for he would have found himself tongue-tied before her.

The wish of the young ladies was to learn, as distinctly as possible, every thing that passed on that terrible night; and Charles related, with perfect simplicity, every circumstance, except one or two, which he thought would affect their feelings too deeply. He could not help expressing his admiration of the rational and manly courage with which his friend had met so sudden a misfortune.

"We were not surprised at this," said his sister: "we always believed that our brother's strength of mind would prove equal to any occasion, however he might be tried."

"And now," replied Charles, "it has been proved that you were right; and you have the comfort of knowing that he is equal to any trial, for none can now befall him more sudden and more terrible."

"No, indeed," replied Miss Monteath; and she passed her hand over her eyes, as if the thoughts of her brother's misfortune were too painful to be borne.

"I mean," continued Charles, "more terrible *at the time*: for though you will not now be inclined to agree with me perhaps, I do not think it will prove a very great lasting misfortune. I have known many instances of similar deprivations, where usefulness and activity have been very little if at all impaired."

Miss Monteath shook her head.

"I incline to think that my young friend is right," said Mr Franklin. "I believe that the worst is over with thy brother and with his friends. When he becomes accustomed to his new feelings, when he finds that art affords valuable helps to repair an accident like this, when he finds that he can pursue his usual employments without impediment, and that the affection of his friends, especially of the nearest and dearest, is enhanced by sympathy and approbation, I will even say admiration, dost thou not think that he will be happy? I think he may be quite as happy as he has ever been."

"There is one thing more that you have not mentioned," said Miss Monteath, "the acquisition of a new friend."

"True," said the Quaker, "of a friend whose faithfulness was singularly proved during the first hours of intercourse."

Charles became anxious to change the subject, and asked Miss Monteath whether she had any idea how soon her brother would be able to return home.

"Not for five or six weeks at the soonest," she said; and, after a few more enquiries, Charles rose to take his leave.

Meantime, Jane had enjoyed a very pleasant hour with Mrs Franklin. This good lady expressed some fear lest Jane should think her impertinent; but she was really so much interested in her situation and circumstances, that she could not help informing herself, as fully as her young friend would allow, of their manner of living. Jane made no mysteries, for she was well enough acquainted with Mrs Franklin's character to be very sure that it was not idle curiosity which made her take so deep an interest in herself and her brothers and sisters. Mrs Franklin ended by saying, "When I am well, I will come and see thee; but in the mean time, thou wilt bring thy sisters here, I hope. I wish to see them, and we have some fine prints, which will perhaps please Isabella, as she likes such things."

Charles and Jane congratulated each other, as soon as they were alone, on the acquisition of such friends as the Franklins appeared inclined to be.

The following week passed away happily and quietly. The only remarkable circumstance which occurred was a call from Mr Monteath and his daughter. Jane was gratified by this mark of attention from Miss Monteath, and Charles was no less pleased by receiving a short note from his friend. It was as follows.

> "My dear Friend,—
>
> "It is with some difficulty that I have obtained permission to write a few lines to you. The purpose of them is to entreat you to spend a day or two with me on your return to London, if you can spare the time to one who has so slight a claim in comparison with your family. On many accounts I wish to see you; but especially that I may express something of the gratitude and friendship which I feel, but cannot write, and which will remain a weight on my mind, unless you will come to me. Do give me the greatest pleasure I can now enjoy. I hope I am not selfish in urging it. Farewell.

"Ever your grateful friend,—

"Henry Monteath."

Charles had pledged himself to be in London by Wednesday; and he therefore determined to leave Exeter on the Monday morning, and to spend the half of Monday and Tuesday with his friend. His sisters were grieved to lose a whole day of his society, but they made no opposition to his plan, ready, as they always were, to give up their own wishes when the sacrifice was required. Isabella worked hard to finish her little book; too hard, Jane feared, for she did not look well, and was obliged to acknowledge frequently that her head ached. On the Saturday she set to work as soon as she returned from school, and was busy at the last drawing all the afternoon. She completed it just before dark, and her brother and sisters heartily congratulated her on having put the finishing stroke to her work: but she seemed to feel little pleasure; and as she was putting away her pencils, Jane observed that her hand shook violently, and that her face was flushed. Charles gently reproached her for her too anxious diligence; and she owned that she felt very unwell, but she did not think it owing to her laborious application. Jane urged her to go to bed; but she would not consent to lose so many hours of Charles's society, and she persisted in sitting up to tea. She was however unable to eat, and her headache became so violent, and was accompanied with so overpowering a sickness, that she could hold up no longer, and was conveyed to her bed. Jane was very uneasy, but Isabella and Hannah both thought it might be a common sick headache, and persuaded Jane not to send for Mr Everett that night.

At bed-time she was very feverish, and passed a miserable night, and when Jane went to her bedside at four o'clock the next morning, she was terrified to find her slightly delirious. Of course she remained with Isabella, and before breakfast-time she sent to request Mr Everett's attendance, as soon as convenient. At six o'clock she gave her patient some tea, and then Isabella spoke sensibly again; but she was restless, and suffering much from headache.

This was sad news for Charles when he came down to breakfast; and this last day with his sisters promised to be but a melancholy one. Mr Everett came early, and he was most anxiously questioned about his patient. He said that she was extremely unwell certainly; but whether it would prove a short and sharp attack of fever, or an illness of more serious consequence, he could not at present tell. He advised that no one should go into her room except Jane and Hannah, till they could be quite sure that there was no fear of infection. He desired Jane not to think of resuming her employments at his house for a week at least, both because it would be too painful to her to leave her sister, and because he had rather ascertain the nature of the disorder, before he exposed his children to the least risk of infection. This did not serve to make poor Jane less anxious. She sat by Isabella's bedside, trying to keep down melancholy thoughts, while Charles took Harriet and Alfred to church. The whole of the day was spent with them, and he scarcely saw Jane at all. In the dusk of the evening, he was sitting by the parlour window, talking to his little brother and sister, when he saw the postman come up to the door. The arrival of a letter was a rare occurrence, and the first idea which entered Charles's mind was that perhaps a further leave of absence had come to cheer him and Jane, when certainly such a comfort would be most welcome. But his heart sunk when he saw Mr Rathbone's hand-writing on the letter which Hannah brought in. He reproached himself for his ill-bodings as they arose, and he asked himself why he dreaded a communication from one who had been the kindest of friends to him, and he anticipated the shame he should feel if, as was very likely, the letter should contain nothing but kindness. He requested Hannah to bring candles, and then to sit with Isabella, while Jane came down to read her letter, for it was addressed to her. Jane opened it with a trembling hand, and Charles at once guessed its contents when he saw it consisted of only a few lines. He caught it as it fell from his sister's hand, and read as follows:

> "Mr Rathbone is sorry that he was prevented by an unavoidable accident from opening Miss Forsyth's letter till yesterday. Mr R. would have rejoiced to afford substantial assistance to the children of an old friend; but they who can set the romantic whims of unformed judgments against the knowledge and experience of a friend who has passed a long life in the world, prove themselves incapable of being guided by advice, and of profiting by well-meant and willing kindness. Mr R. has therefore only to regret that he can be of no further service, and to hope that Mr and Miss Forsyth will meet with other friends, and will know better how to value and retain them."

Jane had hid her face in her hands, and was sobbing violently, while Charles read the letter.

He was almost choked with emotion.

"My poor Jane," he exclaimed, as he hung over her, "that this cruel letter should have come just now, of all times. What a heart must that man have who could write to you in such a way. I wish he could see you now, that he might repent it as he ought to do."

"O Charles!" said Jane, "remember all his kindness to us."

"Remember it!" cried he, "it will stick in my throat as long as I live. O that I could send him back his bank-notes and his presents, and be free of all obligation!"

"Nay, dear Charles, do not let us be ungrateful because he is hasty. His former kindness is not the less noble because of the present misunderstanding. We must be neither ungrateful nor proud."

"It is plain enough that he never saw you, Jane, or he would have blushed to insult such a nature as yours. I wish he could hear you speaking of his kindness just when it is most painful to remember it: he would feel how little he understands you."

"Never mind what he thinks of me," said Jane, raising her head and attempting to smile. She saw that poor Harriet was in tears, and that Alfred was standing beside her chair with a look of deep concern. They both felt that all seemed to go wrong with them this day, though they knew not the cause of their sister's unaccustomed tears.

Jane threw her arm round Alfred's neck and kissed him again and again. "Never mind," she said again, "what Mr Rathbone thinks of us: we have Alfred safe; we have not sacrificed him; we have done what we think is best for our happiness; and shall we not willingly abide by our choice?"

"Surely we will," replied her brother, "and willingly pay the price of our independence, though it be a heavy one."

"It is a heavy one, indeed," said Jane. "I grieve for you the most, Charles. We can go on living as we have lived, and be only reminded that we once had such a friend by the proofs of his kindness which we see every day. But it is hard upon you, separated from your family as you are, to lose your only friend in London."

"Do not think about that, Jane; I have friends, and can make more. If you are able to get over this pretty easily, we need only be sorry for Mr Rathbone: it must give him great pain to think us really ungrateful. Harriet, dear, come and tell me what is the matter. What makes you cry so?"

"Because you are going away, Charles; and Isabella is ill; and Jane cried so; I am sure something is the matter."

"But Isabella will be better to-morrow perhaps, and Jane is not unhappy now; look at her, she is not crying now. Go and kiss her."

"All will come right again soon, I dare say," said Jane. "Charles will come again some time when we are all well."

"And I shall not go to-morrow now," said Charles. "I cannot leave you so full of care."

"O, Charles! you will, you must go," said Jane. "You have promised, and you must go."

"I could not tell when I promised, that Isabella would be ill, and you so anxious. I cannot turn my back on you at such a time."

"You can do us no good, if you stay, indeed. I must be with Isabella, and Harriet and Alfred will be at school; so you would be of no use, and it would make me uncomfortable to think you were breaking your promise. O, indeed, Charles, this is mistaken kindness."

Charles did not know what to think: he proposed to consult Mr Barker.

"Do," said Jane, "he will tell us what is right."

Charles put on his hat.

"I wonder whether we shall see you again?" said Alfred. "Harriet and I are going to bed presently."

Charles kissed them tenderly. "I dare say I shall see you at breakfast to-morrow," said he: "if not, you will remember all the better what I have been saying to you this evening. You will be grown and altered much before I see you again. I hope I shall be able to love you then as well as I do now, or even better."

Mr Barker was much concerned to hear Charles's little tale of anxieties. He advised him, however, to adhere to his promise respecting his return to London. Charles acquiesced at once in the decision of his friend, and was relieved by the kind promises he received that his sisters should be watched over with as much care as if their brother were beside them; especially that Jane should not be allowed to try her strength too much, in case of Isabella's illness proving long or dangerous. Charles with much emotion bid farewell to his good friend, who said, "I cannot do for you what Mr Rathbone would have done: but you may depend on me as a *sure* friend at least. I hope, for his own sake, that he will come round again: in the mean time we must be more sorry than angry."

"I *was* angry," said Charles, "but Jane made me ashamed of myself: she is as grateful to him as ever, and I will try to remember only his past generosity."

"Jane is a good girl, and will be made all the better by these rubs," said Mr Barker. "However, we will smooth things for her as well as we can."

Charles called at Mr Monteath's to say farewell, and to take a parcel from the young ladies to their brother. He said nothing about his sisters, as he knew Jane had rather be left in quietness, than have her attention to her patient interrupted, even by the kind enquiries of friends. Mr Monteath took down Charles's address, and said he hoped to call on him in London before long; and he earnestly desired that any of the family would apply to him in any case where his advice or assistance could be of service.

As Charles went home he thought with pleasure how his circle of friends appeared to be widening. He who was poor, and could only do good by seizing accidental occasions, he who had, in his own opinion, nothing to recommend him to the notice of his superiors, had gained friends whose present kindness was delightful to him, and on the steadiness of whose regard there was every reason to rely. He and his sister agreed, before they separated for the night, that, though they had some cares, they had peculiar blessings; that, though one friend was unhappily estranged, new and valuable supports were gained: and that valuable as these supports were, there was One infinitely more precious, whose love no error can overcloud, no repented sin alienate; who in sorrow draws yet nearer than in gladness, and sheds his own peace over the hearts which humble themselves under his chastening hand.

It had been arranged that Hannah should sit up with Isabella for the first half of the night, and that Jane should take her place at three o'clock in the morning: as by this means she might see Charles before his departure at five o'clock.

Mr Everett had called again in the evening. He saw no signs of improvement in his patient, and was sorry to observe the great reduction of strength which had taken place within a few hours. He was now pretty sure that the fever would prove a serious one. What he said had given Jane no comfort; but she endeavoured to brace up her mind to meet her cares, and she found, as most in her situation do find, that her strength proved equal to her trial. In a melancholy, but not a restless state of mind, she laid her head on her pillow, and having enjoyed the relief of expressing her cares and fears to Him who alone could remove them, she fell asleep, and continued so, till Hannah called her at four o'clock, instead of three, as she had been desired. Jane afterwards asked her the reason, and good Hannah declared that she could not find in her heart to disturb so refreshing a repose, till it was time to call Mr Charles also.

"Thank you, Hannah," said Jane; "but the next time we divide the night, I must take the first half, and you the last."

Isabella had slept but little, and though not delirious, was restless and uncomfortable. Her mind was full of Charles's departure, and of her wish to see him again. She even wished to get up and meet him at the room door, if Jane would not allow him to breathe the air of the sick chamber. Jane was more prudent, however, than to expose Charles to the risk of infection, and she brought Isabella to be content with a cheerful message of love, which she knew Charles would send. Charles was yet more grieved than his poor sister to depart without exchanging a word or a kiss; for he could not keep off the thought that he might perhaps see her no more. There was no knowing; she might perhaps be no nearer death than the others; but it was a great grief to leave her so ill, and without saying farewell. He sent her a note, however, and promised to write frequently to her, and with this she was obliged to be satisfied.

Never had poor Jane felt the trial of separation so much: the trial itself was greater, and she had no liberty to indulge her feelings. She could not leave Isabella, and she could not give way to tears before her, nor even speak to her of her sorrow. She smiled and spoke cheerfully, though her heart was heavier than it had ever been. Charles was not much happier; but they had both the consciousness of being useful to cheer them, and Charles really expected much pleasure from intercourse with Henry Monteath. He arrived at the well-known public-house by breakfast-time: he had recognised the very spot on the road where the coach was upset, and was himself surprised at the involuntary shudder which the sight of it caused.

Mrs Monteath met him on the stairs, and welcomed him kindly. She said that her son was impatient to see him, and would be on his sofa, and prepared for a long day of pleasure, by the time Charles had finished his breakfast. In the mean time she conveyed to Henry the parcel which Charles had brought from the young ladies.

In answer to his very anxious enquiries, Mrs Monteath said that her son's recovery had been as favourable as possible: this was partly owing to the cheerful state of his mind, of which, she said, Charles would be able to judge when he conversed with him. She said she was surprised every day to find how easy she herself was: but she supposed that the pleasure of witnessing his daily progress, made her unmindful of what her son had gone through, and of the trials and deprivations he yet had to encounter. Charles thought this a very natural and happy thing, and he told Mrs Monteath, what he himself believed, that these deprivations would be much less formidable in reality than in anticipation. Mrs Monteath was an anxious mother, and she asked Charles many particulars about her family: how they were in health and spirits; how they spoke respecting their brother; and many other things. Charles told her all that had passed the evening before, during his visit, and observed that when he mentioned Miss Auchinvole, the friend of the young ladies, Mrs Monteath's countenance expressed peculiar interest. Charles had not much to say about her, for she had scarcely spoken, but he could not help saying how much he had been struck by her appearance and manner. She looked pale and anxious, but she smiled occasionally; and there was a sweetness in that smile which Charles thought must make its way to any heart. He freely told Mrs Monteath what he thought, and far as he was from wishing to learn from her manner any family secrets, he could not help believing from the tears which rose to her eyes, and the mournful smile with which she listened to the praises of Margaret Auchinvole, that the friendship between her and Henry Monteath was of a dearer nature than that in which his sisters bore their part. Charles earnestly hoped that this might be the case, and that when restored to health, a happiness, to which this accident need, he thought, oppose no impediment, might be in store for his friend.

Charles observed that there was much more appearance of comfort in the little parlour now than when he saw it before. Mrs Monteath told him that the people of the house were willing and obliging, and that she had contrived by various means to collect comforts round them, and to make their two rooms fit for the accommodation of an invalid, in preference to hazarding a removal, which might have been dangerous, and which her son dreaded more than any thing. She hoped in another week to remove him to lodgings in a farm-house, about four miles off, and in a month or five weeks to take him home.

When Charles entered Monteath's chamber, he saw him lying on his sofa, looking very pale and weak, but with a cheerful countenance. He eagerly held out his hand to Charles, and welcomed him with a smile and words of great kindness. Mrs Monteath left them together.

"I rejoice to see you so much better and happier than when I left you," said Charles.

"Much better and much happier," replied he. "I am glad that you have seen me again; for I am sure all your thoughts of me must have been melancholy thoughts; and I wish that my friend should see me in other hours than those of weakness and misery."

"So far from having none but melancholy thoughts about you," said Charles, "I have been drawing a very fine picture of your future usefulness and happiness, for your sisters' consolation."

"And did they believe you?"

"I hope so, for I am sure I said nothing unreasonable."

"And did they all hear you?"

"No, only two of them that evening. Last night, however, I saw the whole party, and they were all well and happy, as I dare say they have told you themselves."

"They have. When we get to our lodgings in the country next week, some of them will come to us. Much as I long to see them, I almost dread stirring."

"O you will recover much faster when you are in quiet, and when you can go out every day. You can hardly feel here the delight of returning health. I know from experience that the first sight of the face of nature, in a season like this, after days and weeks of illness, is one of the most exquisite pleasures that life can afford."

"*I* believe it," said Monteath. "I expect to enjoy it much; though, with me, all cares will not be over when health returns. I have already made up my mind to every thing, however, and am determined to make the best of my lot. It is astonishing how soon one's mind becomes reconciled to circumstances. At this hour, a fortnight ago, I should have shuddered at the very thoughts of what I have yet to go through: but I am pretty well reconciled to it now, and do not see why I should not be tolerably happy. To be sure, this fortnight has seemed longer than any year of my life before."

"I do not see," said Charles, "why you should not be *very* happy, when you have once got into the round of your occupations again. In the mean time you will meet with some painful circumstances no doubt;

but then you have consolations which have supported you in a far worse trial than any you are likely to meet with again."

"True; those consolations are worth any thing: it makes me quite ashamed to set my fears and troubles in opposition to such comforts."

"If it is not painful to you," said Charles, "I should like to know what your fears and troubles are; and perhaps by bringing yourself to speak frankly of them, you may find that your imagination has magnified them."

"It is selfish to talk so much about myself," replied Monteath.

"I came on purpose to hear you," said Charles, "and nothing can interest me so much."

"Well, then," said Monteath, "I have been thinking how far my usual pursuits will be hindered by this accident. I am afraid that my father will not allow me to take on myself, as I used to do, the most laborious part of our business concerns. I have, to be sure, spent a great part of my time in the counting-house; but there is a great deal of active business to be done besides, and journeys to be performed; and I am afraid that my father will take more upon him than at his age he can do without fatigue."

"I do not see," said Charles, "why you should not be almost as active as you have ever been; and as to journeys, unless this accident has made a coward of you, which I do not believe, you seem to me just as able to take them as ever. If not, it is no difficult matter to procure a traveller. Depend upon it, your father will spare himself for his children's sake. So you see business may go on as well as ever. Now for pleasure. Do you keep a horse?"

"No, but I mean to do it now; that is no difficulty. There is one more, which I am almost ashamed to mention; but I will. I never could bear to be conspicuous, to be unlike other people, to attract notice; in short, to be stared at."

"Do not be ashamed of feeling that," said Charles: "in my opinion, this is the worst evil of all."

"Is it, really?" said Monteath. "Worse than having one's usefulness and independence impaired?"

"No," replied Charles. "But I see no reason why your usefulness and independence should be impaired. If you had lost an arm, the case would have been different: but art affords such helps in your case, that it is only on occasions of extraordinary danger that you would not be able to exert yourself as well as ever."

"I hope you are right," replied Monteath. "You think, then, that I am not wrong to dread being made an object of curiosity for the first time in my life?"

"I do not wonder at it, certainly," said Charles: "but, remember, it will be only a temporary inconvenience: your acquaintance will soon get accustomed to the sight of you; and, if you will condescend to take pains at first with your manner of walking, there will be nothing remarkable in your appearance. I conclude you will throw aside your crutches as soon as you can?"

"Of course," replied Monteath. "You will see me in London for that purpose as soon as I am allowed to go. Now do you think me weak for dwelling on these trifles, as some people call them?"

"Trifles they are not," said Charles: "and therefore it is any thing but weakness to bring them out, to face them, and make up your mind how they are to be met. In my opinion, a great deal of mischief is done by calling these things trifles, and putting them out of sight as fast as possible, instead of affording that help to those who suffer under them which is largely dispensed on occasions which have not nearly so great an effect on happiness."

"That is exactly what I have often thought lately," said Monteath. "In how many books, where the loss of fortune is described, the minutest difficulties which such a loss occasions are detailed at length! but if, as seldom happens, the loss of a limb is mentioned, we never get beyond the first part of the story, and the little daily difficulties and privations, which are of more importance than the lesser evils of poverty, are quite left out of sight. I imagine there are some ideas of ridicule attached to them."

"Perhaps so," replied Charles; "but such associations are false, and ought to be broken through. Blindness is frequently made interesting in books: deafness seldom or never. There are interesting and poetical associations connected with blindness; ridiculous, low, or common ones only with deafness. A blind heroine is charming; but would not all the world laugh at the very idea of a deaf one? And yet this seems to me unjust: for I question whether, in daily life, both would not have an equal chance of appearing ridiculous on some occasions, and interesting on others."

"Do you mean partial or total blindness and deafness? A heroine totally blind is certainly thought more interesting than one partially deaf: but would not a deaf and dumb person make a better figure than one extremely short-sighted?"

Charles laughed. "They are both as far from picturesque as need be, certainly," said he: "but still I think blindness has the advantage in exciting interest."

"Well," said Monteath, "nobody is likely to make a hero of me. I am in no danger of finding my own likeness in a novel or on the stage."

"No," replied Charles, "nor yet in books of any other kind. If you had lost a friend or your fortune, you might find the most exact directions how to comfort yourself, and plenty of medicine of the soul to suit your particular case. As it is, you must look in books for general consolation, and elsewhere for what more you may need."

"This is no desperate condition to be in either," said Monteath. "I think I could do without the general consolations you speak of. I have been on my sofa here this fortnight, with only one book (which of course you mean to except) and my own mind to draw consolation from, and I have found enough for my need. I expect, however, to be in greater need hereafter."

"Surely not," said Charles. "Surely you have gone through the worst!"

"I know not," said Monteath. "The colour of my whole future life has perhaps been changed by this accident; and I must expect this conviction to come upon me painfully from time to time."

"What do you mean?" said Charles. "The whole colour of your future life! You surely do not mean that you will not marry?"

"That is what I was thinking of, certainly," said Henry, in a very low voice.

"My dear friend," said Charles, "this is the scruple of a sick man's brain. Put it out of your head for the present, I advise you, and I will answer for it that, six months hence, you will feel very differently. The woman would but little deserve you who could raise such an objection; and you have just as much power now as ever to make a wife happy."

Charles wished to turn the conversation, for he saw that his friend was agitated; but he could think of nothing to say at the moment, except about Miss Auchinvole, and that was the only subject which would not do. At length he said, "You must not let me weary you with talking. You know I cannot tell what you are equal to, and Mrs

Monteath will never forgive me if I set you back in the least. Had I not better leave you?"

"O no! do not go!" said Monteath; "you do not know how strong I am. I shall sleep in the afternoon, but I hope to have you with me all day besides. I do not scruple saying so, for I cannot conceive that you will find amusement elsewhere in a place like this."

"If I could," said Charles, "I am not much inclined for it to-day. Conversation with a friend is a great cordial in times of anxiety, and I own that I am anxious now."

He said this for the purpose of drawing his friend's attention from a subject which appeared to agitate him too much. Charles was not wrong in expecting his ready sympathy. Isabella's illness was mentioned, and Monteath forgot himself in his anxiety for Charles. He asked many questions about the girls and Alfred.

"How old is Alfred?"

"Nearly eleven."

"What do you intend him for?"

"We have no present intentions about his future destination," said Charles. "He will remain at school till he is fifteen; so we need be in no hurry about it."

"Then your sister will continue on her present plan till that time?"

"Yes," replied Charles; "for Harriet will not be old enough to go out before five years from this time. Isabella wishes to be independent in two years, and I think she will be well qualified; but it will be a grievous thing to Jane to part with her."

"It must, indeed," said Monteath. "You know I have seen your sister Jane, more than once, and she fixed my attention immediately by the way in which she managed those spoiled children of Mrs Everett's. Nobody ever had any control over them but your sister; but they are in much better order than they used to be."

"It gives Jane much satisfaction to think so," said Charles.

"But it must be very discouraging work," said Monteath, "to do her best for them, for half of every day, and to be obliged to surrender them to be spoiled for the other half."

"I should find it so," replied Charles: "but Jane makes as little as possible of discouragements. Her temper used to be an anxious one too: but she has had so much to do and to bear, that she has learned not to look from side to side in hope or fear, but to go on, straight forwards, in the road of duty, whether an easy one or not."

"She is an enviable person then," said Monteath.

"All things are by comparison," said Charles, rather confused when he recollected what he had said about his sister. "I do not mean that she never flags: I was only speaking of her in comparison with myself, and with her former self."

"Nothing but religious principle could enable her to do this," said Monteath. "This is the secret of her superiority, is it not? Without this her trials would have produced depression, instead of renewed energy."

"Certainly," replied Charles. "There are many who pity her under her weight of cares, and who are grieved when they think that she is an orphan, and that she has more arduous duties to perform than many can get through under the guidance and with the assistance of parents or experienced friends. But Jane knows that she is guided, though invisibly, by the best and wisest of Parents, and the Bible is to her as His manifest presence: she has recourse to it on all occasions of difficulty, and can never want confidence or feel forlorn, while such a director is at hand."

"Those whose reason is matured enough, and whose religious affections are cultivated enough to attach their heart and soul to such a guide, may well do without other support," said Monteath. "'The integrity of the upright shall guide them!' But there are few of your sister's age who are thus advanced in the ways of wisdom."

"If so," said Charles, "her superiority is to be ascribed to the peculiar circumstances in which the Father of her spirit has placed her. And, surely, trials which produce such an effect should be endured with submission and remembered with gratitude."

"That comes home to my conscience," said Monteath: "*I* am now under trial, and such ought to be its effect upon me. But your sister's circumstances have been such as to draw her attention from herself, to carry out her affections and fix them on various objects: but I am afraid the direct tendency of personal suffering is to produce selfishness."

"It may either do that or the reverse, I believe," said Charles: "I have known instances of both. I have heard of a cousin of my mother's, who was a cripple from disease. She passed through life very quietly. She never complained of her deprivations: her temper was placid, and she found employment for her cultivated intellect in studies of various kinds: but nobody was ever the better for them. She did no good, though she never did any harm: she never seemed to love any one person more than another, and of course nobody was particularly attached to her. She lived to the age of sixty, and went on with her own pursuits to the very last, but she left no trace behind her of beneficent deeds, and she lived in the memory and not in the affections of those around her. I have always grieved over the wasted talents of this lady. Half her learning communicated to those less informed than herself, half her time (of which she had abundance) devoted to the assistance of her neighbours, half her affections exchanged with those who were disposed to love her, would have made her wise instead of learned, useful instead of harmless, beloved rather than served, and mourned rather than merely remembered."

"But she could not have been a pious woman," said Monteath. "A life of selfishness is inconsistent with piety."

"Nobody can say that she was not religious," replied Charles; "because nobody knew what she felt and thought: some say that she must have been pious, or she could not have been placid and contented under her deprivations. I should therefore suppose that she had just enough reliance upon Providence to prevent a naturally cheerful mind from being corroded by discontent: but it is easy to see that she had not those comprehensive views, which teach that the very best of selfish pleasures, those of intellectual cultivation, are to be pursued as a means only, not as an end, and that the grand design for which we are created is to diminish continually our concern for ourselves in an increasing love of God and our neighbour."

"I cannot help," said Monteath, "applying cases like these to myself, just now. I want to place as many guides and as many warnings before me as possible. I hope it is not selfish to think of these things with a reference to myself, and to tell you that I do so."

"By no means," replied Charles; "for I imagine that you feel the present time as a kind of crisis in your character. I think you must enter the world from a bed of pain, either better or worse than when you left it, and you are right to make use of all the helps you can."

"Then give me," said Monteath, "some instances of benevolence promoted, of hearts and hands opened by personal suffering. It will do me good to hear them."

Just as Charles was beginning to speak, Mrs Monteath came into the room, and the conversation was turned into a different channel.

Charles regretted this, but she had something quite different to ask her son about. The greater part of the day was spent in cheerful chat, and in reading aloud, which Mrs Monteath proposed, that Henry might not exert himself too much in talking. In the evening the young men were again left alone for awhile, and Monteath asked his friend to read a little to him from the Bible. Charles did so with much satisfaction, and after he had done, Henry tried to express to him what comfort and support their religious exercises had afforded him on his night of suffering. Charles rejoiced to hear him say so, but stopped him when he wished to speak of his obligations and his gratitude. They parted for the night with as warm feelings of interest and esteem as one day could produce, and another confirm.

In the morning they met only for a few moments. They agreed to correspond occasionally, and to look forward to a time, not very far distant, when Monteath's visit to London might give them an opportunity of meeting again. Charles then mounted the coach, and sighed when he thought of the friends he had left behind, and of the small number who would greet him with pleasure on his return to London.

Chapter Four.

When Charles returned to his usual employments, and mixed again with companions who had no peculiar interest in his concerns, he could scarcely for an instant keep his thoughts from dwelling on the home he had left, and his anxiety to know more of Isabella became painful.

He received a letter from Jane the day after his arrival, but the tidings were not pleasant. Isabella was in great danger: her fever ran high, and for many hours she had been delirious. Charles was to hear again by the next post. The next post brought a letter from Mr Barker. Isabella was not better, and Mr Everett thought that if a great change for the better did not take place in forty-eight hours, she could not live. After giving these particulars, the letter continued:

> "Do not be too anxious about Jane: she is surrounded by kind friends; who are willing to help her, but she needs no assistance. She will relinquish the care of her sister to none but Hannah, and never even to her, except when a few hours of rest are absolutely necessary to her. She seems strong in mind and body, quite aware of the danger, and quite prepared for every thing. She has allowed her friends to take charge of Harriet and Alfred: they are with us just now. Mr Monteath and his daughters are much concerned at this illness, and so are the Franklins. Mrs F. shews her kindness in a very acceptable manner. She has sent a dinner ready cooked, every day, to your sister's house, that Jane may have as much of Hannah's assistance as possible. Mr Monteath sent some excellent Madeira, on hearing that wine was ordered, and his daughters have procured foreign grapes and various other luxuries for the invalid. I mention these things to prove to you that your sisters will want no assistance that friends can give, and even at this time it will be a great pleasure to you to be convinced that their worth is appreciated, and that their claims to esteem are allowed.

"We are very sorry for you, Charles, that you must be away just now: but you did right in going at the time you promised, and we will still hope that you will be rewarded by hearing better tidings than I am able to communicate to-day. You shall hear by every post. All your friends here send their love to you, and so do I, my dear boy. Farewell.

"P.S. My wife has just been to your sister's. Mr Everett was there, and he thought he perceived a slight improvement in the state of the pulse and skin. May he be right!"

Charles longed to write to Jane, and this postscript encouraged him to do it. He wrote cheerfully, earnestly hoping that before his letter should arrive, such an improvement might have taken place as should render his expressions of hope not ill-timed. Mr Barker wrote again the next day. Isabella was not worse, perhaps a little better, but in a state of such extreme weakness, that there were yet but very slight hopes that she could get through. After this, the accounts were better for a day or two; the fever was gone, and she had gained a little strength. In two days more, Jane wrote herself, as follows.

"At length, dearest Charles, I can write to you again with my own hand. I could not till yesterday leave Isabella's bedside for an hour. Now, however, she sleeps a great deal, and therefore does not require such constant watching. She is certainly better, much better; but still so weak, that she cannot move a limb. O! I was so glad when her delirium ceased. Weak as she was, she was incessantly attempting to rise, and was never quiet for an instant. Now she lies quite still, generally with her eyes closed, so that we can scarcely tell when she is asleep; but I think she dozes for many hours in the day. She takes very little nourishment yet, but we have got down more to-day than yesterday. Our friends have sent all kinds of delicacies to tempt her, but I do not think she knows one thing from another yet. She opens her eyes: I must go to her. O, dear Charles, she has spoken for the first time since her delirium ceased! I could scarcely understand her. 'Are you writing?' she said. 'Yes, I am writing to Charles, to tell him you are better.'—'My love to him: I *am* better.' 'May I say you are comfortable now?'—'O yes!'

"My hopes have risen much since yesterday; but we must beware of too early hope: there is much to be done yet. I have *trusted* throughout. I have tried to be hopeful, even while I contemplated the danger. Now that things look brighter, let us hope yet more; I need not say, let us be grateful; I am sure you are, and my own heart is now full of gratitude. Farewell.

"Jane Forsyth.

"P.S. You shall certainly hear, in a day or two: if not to-morrow, you may conclude that we go on well."

Slowly, very slowly, Isabella continued to gain strength, and in three weeks from Jane's last letter, Charles allowed himself to dismiss all apprehensions. At that time, Isabella added two lines to a letter of Jane's, to shew that she *could* write, though the almost illegible character of the writing shewed how much even this exertion cost her. This was the signal for Charles to write to her, but he wished first to know the opinion of the bookseller to whom he had taken Isabella's little volume. He called at the shop, accordingly, but could obtain no decided answer. The bookseller approved it, on the whole, and thought it might make a very pretty volume, if he could be certain that it would answer the expense of printing handsomely, and so forth. Charles asked him how soon he could make up his mind: he really could not tell, but Charles might call again in a week. Charles agreed to do so, and said that he should wish to have the manuscript back at that time, or a decisive answer. He was sorry not to be able to give Isabella a more satisfactory account of her book; but he had previously warned her that she would probably have need of much patience.

At the end of another week Charles went again. The bookseller had thought no more of the matter; and Charles, not choosing to be any longer put off in this way, insisted on the manuscript being restored to him, and he could not help sighing as he pocketed it. It was not in the most cheerful mood that he left the shop, and his eyes were bent on the ground as he walked. On turning the corner of a street, however, he looked up, and saw at a little distance, on the opposite pavement, a gentleman approaching, who, he was pretty sure, could be no other than Mr Rathbone. A second look convinced him that it was, and he could not resist the impulse which the sight of his old friend inspired, to run towards him. Mr Rathbone looked full at him, and then turned quickly off the pavement, crossed the street, and pursued his way up another street. Charles was quite certain that Mr

Rathbone had seen and known him, and had deliberately avoided him, and with this conviction a flood of bitter feelings came over him which almost overwhelmed him. He struggled against them, but tears would force their way, and his knees even bent under him. There was a print-shop behind him, and he turned round and leaned against the window, while he tried to recover himself.

This was indeed bitter enmity in return for what he could not even allow to be an offence. This thought—that there was, in reality, no offence, helped to restore his courage, and he was just dashing away the last tear that remained upon his cheek, and turning away from the picture-shop, on the beauties of which he had not bestowed a single glance, when a person at his elbow spoke to him. Charles looked up. It was Mr Blyth, who had purchased Isabella's work-bags and boxes.

"It is a curious thing, is it not?" said he to Charles, "that they should have got that sketch up at a print-shop. You see it is the very same as your sister's drawing, that group of people and all."

Charles looked again, and saw a beautiful print of his favourite landscape, the Bubbling Spring. It was the very same indeed, and the figures exactly copied from Isabella's drawing. They could not be mistaken: there were Jane and Harriet seated on the bank, and Alfred kneeling on a stone, and looking into the basin which was formed a little way below the fountain-head.

Charles uttered an exclamation of surprise.

"Why, did not you see it till I pointed it out?" said Mr Blyth.

"No, indeed," replied Charles.

"Where were your eyes, man? But are you sure that your sister did not copy from this print? You told me it was her own sketch, but you might be mistaken."

Charles explained that the figures represented his sisters and brother.

"Well, it is a singular thing: but if her sketches are thought so good, it is a pity she should waste her drawings on workboxes, which hundreds of people can make as well. I think she might turn her talents to greater advantage. May I ask, whether she has been doing any thing of the kind lately?"

Charles hesitated for an instant whether he should confide to Mr Blyth his anxieties about Isabella's little volume. A moment's thought decided him to be open about it. He knew Mr Blyth very well: he thought he might obtain directions and assistance from him better than from any one else in London. He accordingly said, "I have some of my sister's handiwork now in my pocket. I do not quite know what to do with it. If we were not in the street, I would shew it you and consult you."

"Come in here, then," said Mr Blyth, and he entered the shop, and first bought the print and gave it to Charles, and then was ready to hear what his young friend had to say. When he had heard of the unsuccessful application to a bookseller, he asked his name.

"Is he the only one you have applied to?"

"Yes, at present."

"Then perhaps I can help you. You know Mr — is a great publisher. Well: he is a friend of mine, and, if you like it, we will ask his opinion. He will not, at all events, neglect your business. If the volume is not worth the expense of publication, he will tell you so at once; if it is, he will give you a fair price for it."

Charles was much pleased.

"If you have time," said Mr Blyth, "we will go to him now, for he lives near. I shall be very glad to help you," he added, kindly, "for you look rather too anxious."

Mr Blyth represented to the publisher that it was important to his young friend to know soon the fate of his work. An answer was accordingly promised in a week: and Charles, once more full of hope, took leave of Mr Blyth with many thanks.

The bookseller was as good as his word. When Charles called again, at the end of a week, he received twenty guineas for the copyright of the volume. He was quite satisfied, and it gave him much pleasure to transmit the money to Isabella. Jane told him, in her answer, that she had considered the money as disposed of before it arrived, as both she and Isabella thought that the expenses of the latter's illness ought to be defrayed out of their own little fund. But to her agreeable surprise Mrs Everett had told her that her salary was increased to thirty-five pounds a year. Such an increase as this was quite unexpected, and Jane at first refused to receive it, as she had not attended her charge for some weeks, while she was nursing Isabella. Mrs Everett would not listen to her objection, and thus Jane was able to pay her very moderate surgeon's account without breaking into Isabella's earnings.

Jane also laid before her brother a very important plan which her friends, the Everetts and Monteaths, had been forming for her, when they found that Isabella was really likely to be restored to health. It was proposed that Isabella should be sent to a London school for two years, to perfect her in some accomplishments, and that, on her return to Exeter, she and Jane should take a house in a better situation than their own, where they should open a day-school, on an excellent plan. Mrs Everett promised them three pupils from her own family to begin with, and the Miss Monteaths doubted not that their influence would procure more. Jane liked the plan very much, because she and Isabella would not be separated, and they could still afford a home to Alfred for some years. "I need not," said Jane, "tell you the delightful anticipations which I have for the future, if this plan can really be carried into effect. We two have always dreaded a separation, and considered it as unavoidable; for Isabella only looked forward to going out as a private governess, as soon as she felt she could conscientiously engage to teach, and I always regretted having no definite object in view for myself. Now I have, and I must work harder than ever to make up the many deficiencies of which I am sensible, in my qualifications for teaching. I have had a good deal of experience, and I may in that way prove a help to Isabella, and I have tried to make the most of the two hours which I have daily set apart for study. Still much remains to be done; but two years of application may do much for my improvement. I scarcely think at all about the separation from my sister, so pleasant is the prospect of living together afterwards, and in independence too. One thing, however, rather troubles me. I am afraid Isabella's expenses will be considerable, and a new tax upon the kindness of our friends. I think that our little fund, joined to what I can save from our household expenditure in consequence of her absence, may make up the difference for one year: how shall we manage to raise the rest? Can you put me in any way of doing it? She is to go at Christmas. What a pleasure it must be to you, to think of seeing her so soon! You cannot possibly be much together, but a few happy hours you may enjoy occasionally. If Mr Rathbone indeed—but it is wrong to repine at that one sad circumstance when we are so surrounded with blessings. Never, never let us forget to whom we owe them: never again let us repine at the present, or fear for the future. I almost fancy that I can see the time, dearest Charles, when you may begin to work for yourself. If Isabella and I get forward as our friends hope we may, Alfred will be the only remaining charge, for Harriet will be first our pupil, and afterwards our partner, we hope. Tell me, without delay, what you think of our plans."

Charles was much pleased with the scheme, and, before Christmas arrived, he was able to send his sisters the delightful intelligence, that he could assist as well as approve it. Mr Gardiner had given him a situation of greater trust, with an enlarged salary, so that he found he should henceforth be able to spare twenty pounds a year to his sisters. This removed Jane's anxiety with respect to the increased expense which must be incurred by Isabella's London advantages. Still she was afraid that Charles denied himself necessary comforts, and was not satisfied till Isabella had seen his lodgings, and ascertained by close examination that his self-denial was not too severe. His little parlour was found to be the picture of comfort. His sisters had compelled him to accept a share of the beautiful books with which Mr Rathbone had presented them, and he had added a few from time to time, till his little shelves made a very pretty figure. A few of Isabella's sketches and the print which Mr Blyth had given him, ornamented the walls, and his careful landlady was scrupulously neat, as to the furniture of his parlour; so that he was by no means ashamed to let his sister see his little dwelling.

He had another visitor too, about the same time. Henry Monteath had gone to London, according to his plan, and as he was detained three weeks, he and Charles had many opportunities of meeting. Monteath had quite recovered his health, and, what was better, his spirits. He seemed quite happy, took pains to obviate, as far as he could, all inconveniences which arose, and bore cheerfully those deprivations which could not be avoided. He soon walked very well with his new leg, and was so active and strong, that Charles asked him whether he expected to be pitied any more, and if he did, on what account. Monteath replied, that the misfortune was no great one, to be sure, but that no one but himself knew how many and how various had been the little trials he had had to go through since he had last parted with Charles. They were over, however, and he hoped had produced their proper effect, as he certainly felt the wiser for them. Charles was encouraged by his manner of speaking to ask whether he still thought that this accident had changed the colour of his whole future life. Monteath smiled, and said that his fears had misled his judgment, in a case where his interest had been too strong to let him judge impartially. Charles rejoiced at this, and longed to hear something of Miss Auchinvole. Monteath did not mention her at that time, but at another he asked Charles how much he had seen of her during his visit to Exeter. She had returned to Scotland in the autumn, and Monteath was to take two of his sisters to spend some time with her the next summer.

Charles afterwards expressed his obligations to the Miss Monteaths, for the kind interest they had taken in his sisters' plans. Henry would hear no thanks, but asked whether any thing was yet in view for Alfred, and on learning that there was not, said that his father and he had been thinking that they should like to secure the services of a youth so well brought up, under their own eye, and that they proposed to take him, at the age of fourteen, into their warehouse. They would require no premium, but would qualify him for business, and accept his services for five years, during which time he could live with his sisters, and they would then take care to provide him with a responsible and profitable situation in their own establishment. Charles's pleasure in this prospect was inexpressible, and he more than ever rejoiced that he had declined Mr Rathbone's offer. If he had given his wishes full scope, he could not have framed a more delightful scheme. The prospects of his family seemed brightening before them. In two years more they would perhaps be independent, and if Charles had been in the habit of thinking much of himself, he might have added that in seven years he might begin to work for himself: but neither were his own interests important objects with him, nor did he think it wise to look forward very far, knowing as he did how many things might intervene to frustrate plans and destroy hopes, in the course of seven years.

Chapter Five.

In two years from the time that Isabella went to London, she returned from school, improved in appearance and manners, well qualified for assisting Jane in the management of their new establishment, and, though aware of the importance of the situation she was to fill, as simple, affectionate, and sweet-tempered as ever. All was in readiness for them to set out on their new way of life after Christmas. Jane and Mr Barker had fixed on a pleasant small house, in a good situation, in the middle of the city. Jane was sorry to be obliged to take so important a step as engaging a house, without either Charles's or Isabella's sanction; but with such a friend as Mr Barker at hand, her choice could not be much amiss. Happily, Charles was allowed the seasonable pleasure of a week's holiday at Christmas, and he accordingly visited his sisters after they had removed, and just before they opened their school. The arrangement of the house pleased him much. The large school-room was ornamented with their pretty little library, and with a very handsome pair of globes, which Mr and Mrs Everett had presented to Jane as a parting gift, when she quitted the situation in their family which she had filled with so much credit to herself and satisfaction to them. The little parlour was fitted up with plain new furniture, which had been purchased with the remains of the funds which the friends of the young people had raised for their education, on the death of their father. One year's schooling for Alfred was all that remained to be defrayed, as Harriet was to receive the rest of her education from her sisters, and Mr Barker thought that what was left could not be better applied than in the purchase of furniture for the parlour and school-room. The twenty-five guineas which the girls had themselves earned was the means of procuring them a good piano-forte; a thing which was quite necessary in their new establishment, but which could not at present have been afforded if their own industry had not given them the means.

Their number of pupils was at first ten, and they wished to increase it to twenty. The school hours were from nine till three; an hour being allowed in the middle of the time for a walk in fine weather, and play within doors when it rained.

By this means, Jane and Isabella secured the whole afternoon and evening to themselves, and their purpose was to devote a portion of it regularly to their own improvement. If they could obtain the appointed number of scholars, their income, though small, would be amply sufficient for their wants, without any assistance from Charles. He would not hear of this, but insisted on their accepting twenty pounds the first year, and afterwards ten pounds a year for Alfred, till he too should become independent.

It may be imagined with what pleasure Charles saw his sisters thus established, and with how much gratitude he looked on their present situation and future prospects. These feelings were confirmed by a letter which he received from Jane a few weeks after she had begun to experience the toils and satisfactions of school keeping.

> "Our employments," she said, "afford just the anxieties and pleasures which we expected from them. I find less fatigue in my present duties, arduous as they are, than in my situation of daily governess, and Isabella is indefatigable. The children are very fond of her. She seems peculiarly fitted to engage their affections, and that is the grand point of all. We have difficulty in establishing sufficient order and quietness, without introducing formality, which, of all things, we wish to avoid; but in time we hope to get over this, and all our other little difficulties. Our difficulties are all *little* ones now, and the delightful consciousness of independence which attends us, animates all our exertions, and makes every day pass happily.
>
> "We feel as if a great weight were taken off our minds, now that we are at liberty to use our powers for our own support, instead of being burdensome to others. You have long known and enjoyed this feeling; to us it is new and inexpressibly delightful. For the future we have no fears, and no further desires than to go on living as we are living now, only with the additional satisfaction of seeing that our endeavours to be useful are not in vain. Think what it will be, dear Charles, to send our pupils into the world with firm principles, cultivated minds, and amiable manners, fitted to perform their duties, and to do good in their turn. Is not this a satisfaction worth working for? Is not this an end worthy of all our pains, of the employment of all our powers in its accomplishment? Our heavenly Father has blessed us in various ways, in so many that it makes my heart swell with gratitude to think over the few years of

our orphan life, and our present situation: but surely, if He makes us the means of administering religious and moral blessings to others of His offspring, his *last* will be his *best* gift. If we can always feel this, we shall be always happy; but we must not expect that it can be so. We shall meet with much disappointment: we shall have to lament the ill success of our labours in some instances, and, in all, shall feel occasional humiliation that we have not done more, instead of complacency that we have done so much: besides, there is a kind of ardour and enthusiasm in us just at present, which will subside in some degree after a time, and make us more painfully aware than we are now, of the difficulties and labours of our employments. We are, however, abundantly happy at present, and full of hope for the future.

"One reason why I write to you to-day, instead of at the regular time, is, that you may know, as soon as possible, that Alfred has gained great honour at the school examinations this week. He has taken his place pretty high in the next class, and when Mr Barker called on Mr —, to settle the school-account, he was pleased to hear very high praise of Alfred. Mr Monteath is very kind to him: he asked him to dinner last week, and made him very happy. Alfred likes the idea of being in the warehouse much, and I am glad he knows what he has to look forward to. I have heard, through the Miss Monteaths, of two more pupils who are to come to us at Midsummer, and Mrs Franklin has told us that an application is about to be made for another, at the same time, from a friend of hers: so we are likely to begin with fifteen next half-year.

"Mr and Mrs H. Monteath return from Scotland in a week or two. Their house is very near ours, and they have frequently expressed a wish that we may be good neighbours. This will be a great privilege to us and to you in your occasional visits. I think you will henceforth be able to come once a year, and it is possible, that if we go on prosperously, you may see us in London some time or other. We have no plan at present for any thing of the kind; but it would certainly be a great advantage to Isabella to have lessons from London masters occasionally. This, however, must be left to the future to arrange. In the mean time, we are very happy that so many of us have been allowed to live together. I once thought that we should be all dispersed: you where you are; Isabella as a private governess; Alfred in India; and myself—I did not know where. But now four out of five of us are living under one roof, and with no fear of being separated. O what a privilege! But I must stop my pen. I sat down intending to shew you how happy we are. Have I succeeded? If I have, join me in thanksgivings to the 'Father of the fatherless,'

"I am your most affectionate,—

"Jane Forsyth."

Finis.